LONELINESS:
the fear of love

IRA J. TANNER

harper & row, publishers

new york, evanston,

san francisco, london

To my wife, June, four daughters, Kathy, Connie, Kristi, and Mary Beth, each of whom could probably write a book on loneliness/aloneness as a result of the time that I have spent apart from them during the writing of this book.

STANDARD BOOK NUMRER: 06-014218-9

LIBRARY OF CONGRESS CATALOG CARD NUMBER: 72-9158

contents

preface

In addition to my private counseling practice, in recent years I have been associated with the Institute for Transactional Analysis in Sacramento, California, founded by Dr. Thomas A. Harris, who is also the president of the Institute. Some of you familiar with this new approach in the field of human communication may recognize some of the language of Transactional Analysis as it is applied to the disease of loneliness. For others it will be an introduction.

I am indebted to a number of colleagues with whom I have worked over the years: Dr. Harris, Dr. Gordon Haiberg, vice-president of the Institute, Marc Kluender, and Russell Osnes. Some of the insights in this book have evolved out of my contacts at the Institute. For the most part, however, they have come in working with individuals in my private practice. Some of them who knew that I was writing this book have been very helpful in both writing and verbalizing their loneliness feelings and experiences. With their permission, but without the use of their real names, some of what they shared with me is included here.

All the problems that patients have brought to me and everything that has happened in my life over the last twenty years have pointed not only to the writing of this book but to the topic that I chose—my career, my many and changing relationships and, not least of all, a seasoning that only passing years can contribute. The fact, then, that I chose loneliness as my topic was not just accidental.

IRA J. TANNER

introduction

After a plumber spent about two minutes in repairing the furnace in a house in suburbia, he told the homeowner the bill would be $30. The irate breadwinner proceeded to launch into a verbal tirade that covered a broad range of "awfuls"— from inflation to the plumber's dishonesty. "You just looked at my furnace and hit it *once* with your hammer!" he stormed. "That's right," replied the plumber with cool confidence. "I charged you $5 for the visit and $25 for knowing where to hit." He collected.

We dole out hefty chunks of money to people for knowing where to hit, even if it is sometimes but one blow of the hammer. It is the same with the vast assortment of human ills, whether they are emotional, physical, or spiritual in nature.

But with the disease of loneliness we have not always known where to hit. Loneliness is the single experience most common to all of us yet is also the most misunderstood. Generally, its diagnosis, if there is one, is often vague or downright misleading. Today huge throngs of people are suffering from the disease and going untreated because they are not aware of the nature of their ailment. Until the problem is understood and correctly diagnosed there can be no effective prescription for its cure.

One reason the disease has now reached epidemic proportions is that it is frequently hidden under the disguise of many other experiences in life. If we insist on calling loneliness everything else but what it really is—LONELINESS—we will continue to fumble for a cure.

Sometimes we apply the word loneliness to nostalgia and melancholy. But they are not one and the same thing. We also use it to describe the feelings that accompany particular seasons of life, especially old age. Our greatest mistake is in not distinguishing between "aloneness" and "loneliness." Our periods of aloneness, if simply allowed to happen, to be experienced by ourselves, can be among the most rewarding of our lives. It *is* possible to be alone and not be lonely.

We are lonely because of our fear of love. One man said skeptically, "Afraid of love? You've got to be kidding. How can people be afraid of the one thing that makes the world go round—something every man, woman, or child wants the most? It doesn't make sense." I concur. Intellectually it does not make sense. Somehow it makes more sense if we say that we are afraid of snakes, high places, or maybe the terrifying tilt-a-whirl at the fairground. But to fear love? It's like hearing someone announce, "The tastiest topping on ice cream is mustard." To some, therefore, it makes no sense to say that a fear of love and loneliness are identical. Yet, whenever we risk saying to anyone that we are lonely we are claiming just that, as illogical as it may sound. It is because the two words *fear* and *love*, used together, have seemed so incompatible that we have not always understood loneliness for what it really is.

"Sometimes," said a divorced woman who had chosen to work the graveyard shift as one way of dealing with her loneliness, "there are degrees of loneliness for me within a given day. I can feel a little afraid of love in the morning, but in the afternoon—in a different setting and with different people—my fear escalates into sheer terror and I panic."

Our understanding of loneliness depends mainly upon the perspective from which we view love. We see it usually from four different vantage points.

"I don't deserve to be loved and I'll prove it." I'M NOT OK—YOU'RE OK

"I don't trust people who want to give love and I'll prove it." I'M OK—YOU'RE NOT OK

"I've given up trying to give it or receive it." I'M NOT OK—YOU'RE NOT OK

All these three life positions are underscored by a fear of love. Our hope lies in the fourth position: I'M OK—YOU'RE OK. After living in it for longer periods of time, we begin to rise above our fear of love and gradually move away from our basic loneliness.

The nature of our fear of love is also shaped by our belief concerning the basic nature of man: Is it "good" or "evil"? Spelled out most forcefully in religious belief, particularly by the doctrine of man as sinner, the fashion in which loneliness and religion are linked together is discussed in Chapter 11 of this book.

The reason that many of us never even begin to break away from the grip of loneliness is that we insist on making others responsible for our individual fears of love. This may have been natural when we were helpless, dependent little people. But in playing the role of victims beyond childhood it is possible to go through life merely *reacting* to other people and events, never assuming personal responsibility for *acting*. Where that is the case, loneliness is of our own doing.

The vast majority of Americans now live in metropolitan areas. Seventy percent of us live on 2 percent of the land. It almost looks as if coming together were the answer to loneliness. It is not. Being with people gives us no immunity to the disease. Often in fact, when surrounded by people, the fear of love already present in us can be aggravated to the point of despair, panic, or even deeper loneliness.

Loneliness knows no boundaries. It is felt by the rich and the poor, the famous and the unknown, the married and the single, male and female, children and the aging, in the city or in the prairie village. "It doesn't happen just on dark days," novelist Faith Baldwin points out. "It can pierce you like a knife on a spring morning or on a golden summer afternoon— wherever you are and whatever you are doing." Reflecting on its dogged, underlying persistence, a hospital patient commented, "Loneliness is always there, waiting to take over, and when it does it is really hard to get rid of. It takes work—a real struggle, really fighting back."

One of the greatest revelations to me as a marriage and family counselor has been the discovery that the most intense loneliness is found within the home and family, where communication is in the process of breaking down or is already in a shambles. Behind lack of communication there is almost always a fear of love; a fear that is expressed in many different attitudes and modes of behavior.

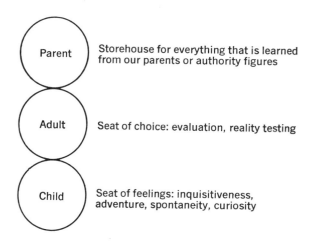

Parent — Storehouse for everything that is learned from our parents or authority figures

Adult — Seat of choice: evaluation, reality testing

Child — Seat of feelings: inquisitiveness, adventure, spontaneity, curiosity

The simplistic language of Transactional Analysis provides us with handles by which we can more easily understand personality and communication. The Parent–Adult–Child concept of personality is particularly applicable to the disease of loneliness. *The posture of the Not OK Child within each of us is one of fear, a fear that manifests itself most readily in feelings of loneliness.*

In what follows, the nature of the problem will be traced from childhood through the various stages of life.

1 we start out lonely

"It is loneliness that makes the loudest noise. This
is as true of men as of dogs."
—ERIC HOFFER

In our town, when you pick up the telephone receiver and dial a certain number, there is a momentary silence before a pleasant, recorded female voice routinely announces: "The time is . . . " The telephone company may or may not be aware of it, but there are those who constantly dial that number, who are not even remotely interested in the time but need only to hear a voice; settling grimly for a recording that spews out in staccato fashion something as impersonal as the time of day. One such person, reflecting the feelings of many others, comments: "I have felt so intense a need to hear the sound of an adult human voice, especially during the lonely hours of the night, that I have dialed the time and just listened to it for a while. This helps at first but then I feel shame for having to resort to such a thing." Without a doubt there are other people in other towns today, whose fear of love has placed them in predicaments so painful that they, too, are resorting to (and temporarily settling for) such pathetic devices as telephoning a recording or turning on the radio to keep in contact with other human beings.

Loneliness. The word itself, perhaps more than any other word in the English language, has a mournful, if not eerie, sound to it. Someone old, sitting on a park bench, long-faced, watching young people and life pass by? Maybe. But it could also be someone who is always first to volunteer his services as coach for a Little League team; someone in the senior high school class who is voted the most likely to succeed; salesman of the month or man of the year. "Nervous breakdown—exhaustion—collapse." Such cases are rarely diagnosed as being rooted in a fear of love but frequently are rooted in just that and not in overwork, given as the excuse. It fells those people who often seem to be its least likely candidates, because they are always surrounded by people. We react, "Anyone but Bob," upon hearing the news that he has been confined to the psychiatric ward of a local hospital. "Why, he's always the life of the party, the first to come, greeting everyone at the door, and the last to leave." There are a lot of people like Bob who, driven by a fear of love and loneliness, exceed their physical and emotional limits in an effort to make themselves lovable to everyone.

Consider the case of Evelyn, a stylish woman in her early fifties, three times divorced. "What's wrong with me, anyway," she mumbles with monotonous repetition through an alcoholic haze. Scarred by the pain that can be caused by human interaction, she has gone through the misery of having loved and lost many times. Bewildered by her persistent need to drink, she was unaware that she had made a decision somewhere back along the way: "Loving just isn't worth it. I can't risk being hurt any more." Her dilemma—an agonizing fear of love, yet a still present need for it that she could not drown with alcohol—was symbolized by an obedient parakeet named David, which was housed in an elegant cage by the couch. She had trained him to say upon command, "I love you." David was the only living being from whom she chose to hear the words. Her parakeet was a safe object of love; he would not hurt or reject her.

Our root loneliness: when it begins

The person who says "I am never lonely" either does not understand the meaning of the word or is fooling himself. This book does not want to make people feel lonely who are not aware of loneliness. But it does say that loneliness is something that we all have to deal with, at one time or another, in our lives. There are no privileged few and no immunization against the disease. In fact, without exception, *every little person is lonely*. Loneliness has its beginnings in childhood sometime between the ages of one and three. It is a root condition of life and it is during these post-embryonic years that we first begin to experience *doubt* as to our self worth.

Some people are lonelier than others. The feeling hinges on the intensity of our fear of love. This is not an indictment of any of us; it is not a sign of weakness. But to do nothing about it is irresponsible. Something can always be done about loneliness.

The little person, though he often *feels* rejected, is rarely *actually* rejected. Feeling rejected is the unfortunate state of childhood. When he or she reaches out for love and it is not returned, the child does not understand intellectually the reasons for the lack of response; indeed it *cannot*. It could well be that mother and father were too busy (or thought they were), felt unwell, did not hear or notice, or were themselves afraid of love. But the only manner in which the little person can interpret this lack of response is to doubt his own self worth—concluding that there must be something about him that is unlovable. As these incidents mount and his doubts increase, he begins to experience the first tinges of fear. In addition, he is discovering that whenever he reaches out for love there is *risk;* sometimes the response meets his needs, at other times it is woefully inadequate. And if he lives to be seventy-five, that will still be the case. With loving, there is always risk.

Ultimately, between one and three years of age, in his desperate effort to dispose of the persistent seesaw battle within him, "Am I or am I not lovable?," he arrives at the firm conclusion, "I am not lovable."

It all began with doubt as to his own self worth and through his inability to reason intellectually resulted in an erroneous view of his self worth based upon his fear of love.

H. L. Mencken summed it up: "The one permanent emotion of the inferior man is fear." Because feelings of inferiority, based upon a fear of love, are a basic condition of childhood, no one escapes loneliness.

How root loneliness is compounded

Of itself, our root loneliness would be painful enough. But like a blister on the heel that is aggravated and rubbed raw by a shoe, so conditions and situations in life have a way of continually rubbing our loneliness raw, intensifying our fear of love. As the child grows older, asks more questions, and expresses his individuality in the form of adventure, inquisitiveness, curiosity, and spontaneity, adults unwittingly apply value judgments to what he expresses. This further accentuates his root loneliness. He may be told that his anger is inappropriate, that his fears are a sign of weakness, or that his crying and sadness reflect a character lack. Much to his dismay, certain aspects of his inquisitiveness, in the form of questions, are branded as dirty, stupid, or childish, making him wonder: "Does it really pay to think for myself?"

Children are also peppered with an assortment of slogans, injunctions, and orders, most of which center on the words DON'T, ALWAYS, NEVER.

Don't start anything you can't finish
Don't waste anything
Don't ask questions; do as you're told (there is no such word as can't)
Don't drink out of the refrigerator water jar
Don't talk to strangers
Don't ever let me hear you say that again
Don't run away from a fight
Don't come home crying again
Don't talk with your hands
Don't trust Christians
Don't take gum from anyone; it might have Spanish fly in it
Don't masturbate, or your penis will shrivel and fall off
Don't run, it isn't ladylike
Don't whistle, it isn't ladylike
Always wear good underwear when you take a trip; you might get in an accident (figure that one out)
Always say "thank you," "yes, sir," and "no, sir"
Always wipe the toilet seat before you sit on it
Always complete your homework before playing
Always be polite to Mother's friends
Always keep your hands to yourself
Always be kind to animals
Always keep your knees together
Never turn and look at anyone in the street
Never forget that cleanliness is next to godliness
Never forget that people are watching you
Never take food or candy from a stranger
Never touch little girls
Never forget to write your mother once a week
Never charge anything; always pay cash

Add to these such gems as, "I hope you have ten kids as bad as you are," "Boys are after just one thing . . . sex" and, "Don't make faces in the mirror or your face will stay that way," and it isn't surprising that these snowballing value judgments gradually lead the child to conclude that his person has two sides—a good side and a bad side, or a weak side and a strong side. What he concludes to be his bad side will be the thoughts and feelings that he has expressed to others, who have strongly disapproved of them. His good side becomes the side that others have praised and accepted. This accentuates his fear of love and he concludes that if he is to remain in the good graces of his parents and not be cut off from their love, he will have to try to abandon his "bad" or "weak" side.

But what he abandons "hurts" because he blunts parts of his inner Natural Child. It is at this point that his inner Adapted Child comes into the picture.

What he stops expressing, out of fear, are the parts of him that were the most delightful—much of his curiosity, spontaneity, daring; probably his anger and even his joy.

A prominent civic leader expressed it well. "Something of *ME* is missing. I've tried for so long to make myself lovable to everybody in this community that I have lost complete

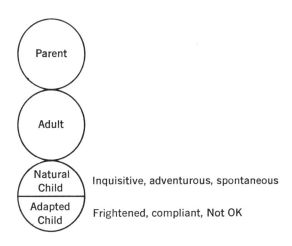

touch with what at one time *felt good to me*, what it was I enjoyed doing."

It is much like a phonograph record whose hole is not quite on dead center. Being slightly off, the needle is not in harmony with the grooves on the record and the words are garbled. All the fears experienced in frantic efforts to make ourselves lovable result in an inner shift within the little person. The natural flowing manner in which he *would* spontaneously respond to outside stimuli gradually gives way to the manner in which he feels he SHOULD and MUST respond if he is to keep the love of his parents. Inner disharmony results, and he loses touch with his own central valuing system.

The universal loneliness experienced by children seems to put parents in a bad light. It is as though they willfully batter children into becoming trembling robots, insisting that they become carbon copies of themselves. Parents are frequently self-righteous and prejudiced, communicating both verbally and nonverbally that "my way is the only way" and "don't you ever dare to question my wisdom," but many actions and attitudes of the parents are also nurturing and understanding, with the child's physical and emotional well-being uppermost in their minds.

It is primarily by virtue of the child's helpless and dependent *position* in life that he begins to dissociate himself from his own valuing system. Even if parents responded in an individual way to the child's every expressed need, at times he would still interpret the sound of their voices, posture, a slap on the hand, or the casual manner in which he was being fed, as a sign that he was unlovable. It would be different if he could understand, for instance, that the casual manner in which he was being crooked in his mother's arm was not indicative of her lack of love for him but because it was 2:00 A.M. and that she was hunched over at a 45-degree angle, attempting to test the warmth of the bottle with her other hand. But the child doesn't yet have that kind of data in his Adult with which to work. In his bewilderment there is only one conclusion he can draw: *"Being held like this means I'm unlovable."* Once that interpretation of an external event has been "taped" by the little person, it is recorded permanently in his brain.

"Old tapes" and present loneliness

Our internal Parent is always borrowed from data fed into us at an early age from external sources, i.e., parents and other authority figures. Because the Adult in the little person—seat of choice, evaluation, reality testing, probability estimating, awareness of consequences—does not begin to emerge until about the age of ten months, there is no way in which data funneled into the Parent from outside sources may be objectively analyzed and evaluated. Even after the Adult in the little one is *first* energized, its strength is such that during the first three years of life it is incapable of doing the necessary job in terms of dealing adequately with the overwhelming amount of data in his inner Parent.

At the same time that these external events are being recorded in the brain, our inner Child is *reacting* to these events in a particular fashion. These reactions, in the form of feelings, are recorded in the inner Child and are available for replay at any time in the future. The thing to remember, however, is that most of these reactions are recorded from the perspective of fear in our NOT OK INNER CHILD, hence our loneliness.

The trouble is, having once concluded that the casual manner in which we were being held means "I'm unlovable," we may discover, much to our dismay some ten or twenty years later, that the same old tape begins to roll again when a friend, relative, or lover hugs, holds, or touches us. "Being touched or held in this manner can mean only one thing—I'm unlovable." Panic may mount: "What have *I* done in *this* relationship to make myself unlovable?"

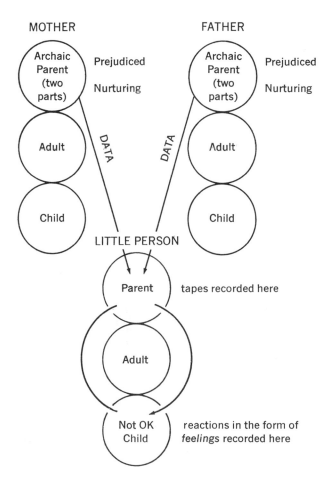

If this happens when our Adult is alert, operative, and in a position to compute the data, it will step in and ask, "Wait a minute—what was the original transaction?" We may not be able to recall the *original* transaction *per se,* the time when we first felt that way, although this is sometimes possible. But even if we cannot, we can be sure, after having checked matters out with our present friend and discovered the friendship to be on firm ground, that our feeling of being unlovable now is just the replay of an old tape—termed a "dialogue"—of our inner Parent and Child. We are assuming the responsibility for our fear of love *now* because we are not placing the blame on present circumstances but putting it "back there" where it rightfully belongs. Hopefully our Adult will be energized to the point that it will be able to turn down the volume on our present fear.

It should be obvious, therefore, that our fear of love with someone in the present is not always the result of something they said or did. Rather, it is that our "I'm not lovable" tape which was recorded way back in time is reactivated in response to an external event; something someone *does or says now;* his tone of voice, the manner in which he shrugs his shoulders, shakes his head, tightens his lips, throws his hands in the air—anything at all. Sadly, when our fears of love out of the past are recalled by such events, we are prevented from appreciating love in the present.

Many who marry impulsively, often on the rebound in the wake of a miserable first alliance, do not take the necessary time between marriages to "update" feeling tapes that were reinforced in that first relationship; hence they are dismayed at the irrational fears of love that develop into something approximating total paralysis in the second marriage. The old inner tape of "I'm not lovable" can roll at the slightest provocation, usually accompanied by a pained moan: "Oh, no, I can't believe it. Here we go again."

There can be difficulty enough if one partner in the relationship is in such straits. But if both partners bear battle scars from a first marriage, then it is like having two hi-fidelity tape recorders blaring from opposite corners of the same room. In my experience, the primary reason for floundering second marriages is that there is an inability or unwillingness to deal NOW with tapes recorded in the first marriage. The volume is too loud, covering everything in the present with suspicion, mistrust, and above all a fear of the risk in both giving and receiving love. Needless to say, if there was loneliness in a first marriage, that loneliness will be twice as painful in the second one.

Symptoms of loneliness

Loneliness has a way of infecting every fiber of our being: our hopes, ambitions, dreams, vitality, desires, wants, as well as our actual physical bodies. Eating and sleeping are frequently affected. Obesity and greed may well be symptoms of loneliness, although a loss of weight can also be traced to despair that goes with a feeling of being of no importance or worth to anyone, not even to ourselves. The misery of loneliness may manifest itself in aches (imagined or real) in the body. Weakness in the legs is not uncommon, stemming from the heavy burden of fear that we are carrying on our backs. Stooped shoulders, turned-down corners of the mouth, a slow and painful walk, silence and withdrawal—all bear testimony to the disease. "I hurt deep down in the pit of my stomach, my arms and shoulders ache to be held tight . . . to be told that I am really loved for what I am," said one woman.

But our eyes tell the truest story. The sadness of our loneliness is frequently most easily detected there. But it is possible to be fooled. Many, like Bob, become expert in putting on a cheerful face, walking erectly, always smiling, perpetually backslapping, "the life of the party." For this reason, it is not wise to diagnose loneliness from any one or combination of the foregoing symptoms *alone*.

Some say that loneliness pain can be more severe than actual physical pain. But there is no medication to ease it, no ointment to soothe the ache. The use of alcohol is an attempt to forget it, but the relief is short-lived, numbing the fear for a while. "Booze doesn't wash away my loneliness," admits one alcoholic. "It only irrigates it temporarily." But again, when its pain becomes unbearable, we will settle for "irrigation." The use of many and varied drugs is also a "solution" that countless millions prescribe for themselves every day, but this also provides only temporary relief from fear. Thousands of Americans commit suicide every year. Many more attempt it.

Our fear of love is difficult to diagnose because from childhood we devise so many ways of coping with it, and cleverly covering it up as well. That mountain of defenses will first of all have to be whittled down. When it is, a fear of love will always be found at the base.

Our central point is: *Fear of love is the root cause of every attitude and form of behavior that separates us from each other.* The most telling sign of our humanness—our fear—is difficult to detect, even feel sometimes, because it is not always characterized by a sudden onset of trembling, sweating palms, or knots in the stomach. Since it is a root condition of life it is an inherent component of our personhood. As we age, our fear of love is masked by many different attitudes and forms of behavior—running away, jealousy, narcissism, snobbery, competing, lying, stealing, and so on. Anger is frequently used to cope with a feared threat, either imagined or real, to our self image.

In counseling with married couples, the initial complaints are usually *surface symptoms* related to a deeper cause, a fear of love.

"He tries to control me."

"She never lets me think for myself."

"He won't listen."

"He's always got to have his own way."

"She doesn't touch me any more."

If the clients do not stop their visits at the point when the fear is about to be uncovered, they learn that their complaints can be invariably traced to a fear of love, that is, giving it or receiving it. Some or all of the element of risk is gone. There are fears of hurting, of being hurt, of misunderstanding or of being misunderstood, of criticizing or of being criticized, of being laughed at, of receiving advice, of appearing awkward, of being judged, and also a fear of crying, offending, rejection, abandonment, and possibly physical violence. One person complained, justifiably, "Whenever I risk sharing my feelings I can predict that in a minute or two my husband will either go to sleep or walk out on me . . . and I can't risk that sort of rejection much longer." No matter from which angle we size it up, a fear of love is the cause of poor communication or no communication at all between people.

Frozen in the middle

My young friend sat on a chair in front of me, slouched over to one side, exhibiting all the earmarks of a twelve-year-old boy, with the evidence of many outdoor adventures on his patched and faded jeans. With his eyes fixed on the floor he spoke in a soft, halting voice. It seems that his dad had left home to live with another woman, leaving his mother, a six-year-old brother, and himself to shift for themselves. Although he related many good feelings about his past association with his dad, there came a moment when he raised his head, looked squarely at me, and blurted out angrily, "But I never want to see Dad again." He started to cry and after his tears had stopped he went on to talk about the visits his younger brother was still making to his father's new home and of his seeming innocence in light of the divorce that had broken up the family. Then he added, "If I were six, like my brother, I wouldn't have to understand. But I'm twelve and I do understand." The pain lay in his awareness of a deep hurt, feelings of rejection, and a fear of taking a risk, yet also wanting to run back into his father's arms again. Caught somewhere in the middle, he had *frozen* into a state of deep loneliness; afraid of the one thing that he most wanted—to love and be loved. When we take all the risk out of love, the only alternative is to "freeze up."

Our loneliness always finds us frozen somewhere *in the*

middle: wanting love but running from it at the same time. It is a kind of death. "I spend quite a bit of time just being *numb,* no, paralyzed," explained one woman who has been lonely ever since she can remember. "I spend a lot of time crying . . . really sobbing. . . . Then I always get a bad headache and that certainly doesn't help." It frequently happens that just at the time the prospects of love are on hand we turn our backs and run in fear, even panic. It's too risky. We cannot be responsible for the personal hurt and feelings of rejection if the gift of ourselves is not accepted and valued for what it is. The less we are willing to risk, the more lonely we become.

Because of this fear of love we painfully and often grudgingly come to settle for being with people in a *physical* sense, yet at the same time are on the lookout for those times when we will be able to take risks and advance beyond the polite and formal niceties in order to love and be loved.

When our loneliness finds us in this frozen state, any movement away from it is best described by the verb "thaw." It isn't that we become less lonely but that our loneliness thaws as we move off dead center.

Loneliness says: "If he got to know me . . ."

"I'm just certain if he got to know me he wouldn't like me . . . would find something to disapprove of . . . would find me unlovable." When *we* decide *for others* in advance of a contemplated friendship that such is "certain" to be the case, we manage, through our fear of love, to maintain the needed and safe distance from people. It is a dandy defense employed by the perennially lonely. But such decisions on our part are also a put-down of people who might thoroughly enjoy our company, and who, if given the chance to become better acquainted with us over a period of time, might just decide that we are really OK people. It is a put-down in the sense that we rob them of the right to make that decision for themselves. But this is just another facet of the no-risk philosophy that we cling to in our loneliness.

Loneliness and roles

As we grow older we notice an uncaring attitude in the world that tends to intensify our root loneliness even more. For all of us this serves to confirm our already established conclusion: "I'm not loved for what I am." Someone, reflecting on the impersonality of life, observed:

To the doctor I'm a patient
To the lawyer—a client
To the editor—a subscriber
To the retailer—a shopper
To the educator—a student
To the manufacturer—a dealer
To the politician—a constituent
To the banker—a depositor-borrower
To the sports promoter—a fan
To the airlines—a passenger
To the minister—a parishioner
To the military—a number or a soldier.

It is apt to make us sad, angry, or frightened. Such labels do not always take into consideration our uniqueness, our talents and abilities. That hurts. These labels are also likely to cause a replay of the old "I'm not lovable" inner dialogue between our Parent and Child. But such impersonality is a fact of life about which we can do very little. Further, we do not want or need the understanding of everyone. To have *one* person who understands, appreciates, and values our individual uniqueness is sometimes enough.

If we feel we do not have one we can give love to and receive love from (in that order) then we are indeed lonely. Frequently, however, such a feeling is based on a decision that we will never risk loving again. One of the premises of this book is that no one ever needs to be in that position. As long as we are willing to risk loving there will always be times when the response fulfills our need to be loved, and our loneliness thaws. These responses may come from people we did not dream would ever respond to us. But that is part and parcel of the risk, indeed the excitement, of loving.

Because it is less risky, we let each other know of our loneliness pain in a number of indirect and shrouded ways:

> I don't feel comfortable around people.
> I wish I knew you better.
> I don't know what to say to people after I say hello.
> I would like to feel closer to you.
> I'm uncomfortable at parties.

All these statements are related to fear; either our fear of love or the fear of others to risk loving us. When we are lonely it is important that we make that distinction.

Few of us admit openly that we are lonely. We hesitate to say it in such a blunt way, not merely because we are frequently unaware of the nature of our "hurt," but because it would make us vulnerable to the judgment of, and misinterpretation by, others; not least of all to be thought weak. At other times we cannot risk disappointing them, for it could very well be that in the past we have worked hard at covering up our loneliness pain with them. In giving the appearance of independence, sureness, and confidence, we have attracted friends (yes, even mates) who were more interested in using us to bolster their own limp egos than in loving us. To say "I am lonely" is to express a need for understanding and love, and at such moments our dependent friends might be shocked, frightened, and feel helpless to do anything about it. Then we may resolve to make new friends who are more interested in understanding and loving us than they are in using us.

It also seems difficult for us to convey the pain of loneliness in words. We try, but somehow words alone cannot adequately convey *feelings*; and loneliness is a feeling. One man, when asked for his definition of it, said, "Loneliness is a feeling and a fact and it has many degrees." For the most part we, as previously explained, refer to it in indirect ways. Loneliness is fear; and fear is a feeling that is difficult to intellectualize, to put into words.

When our fear of love and resulting loneliness mount to panic, we sometimes find ourselves doing things that defy all logic and take on the appearance of the irrational. "I do many things I normally would never do, maybe even unwise things, like stopping strangers and talking to them," said a single woman in her mid-twenties. "Or telling people I barely know some very personal things about myself. This surely isn't wise or logical, and sometimes even results in hurting me. But by now I'm not thinking, really. I only feel real hard, deep, desperate panic . . . and when I'm in that situation I will often do anything . . . not even stopping to think of the possibility of rejection." She continued, "I have gone on long walks and when I have reached a quiet stretch of road, have debated aloud *with myself* some of my feelings and ideas. This really helps, especially when one of my voices sounds mature and confident. But this is a risk, too, since I seem to have gotten into the habit of talking to myself and this really upsets and alienates some people when I tell them."

Situational loneliness

Situational loneliness is related to a time of life that aggravates our present root loneliness. Teen-agers, housewives, and the elderly fall into this category. Because of their situation in life, they may find their loneliness pain multiplied.

A teen-ager explained her situational loneliness in these terms: "I'm too young for dates and too old for Daddy's lap." During the adolescent years, a lessening of physical contact with others contributes to their loneliness pain. Nothing soothes and complements our need for love more than a touch. The sudden curtailment of touching frequently leaves the teen-ager in a state of heightened fear—wanting to be loved in this manner, yet running from it because of feelings of awkwardness and embarrassment.

But their greatest pain accompanies a fear of being misunderstood. We are the most apt to be misunderstood at this time of life. Though teen-agers do not want to share all of their feelings with adults, when they choose to do so it is with the hope that their mothers and fathers will try to understand how they feel; that the gift of themselves will be unconditionally accepted. If it isn't, they will probably withdraw, resolving to be more cautious next time. Over and above withdrawal, the signs of their loneliness are depression, the use of drugs, delinquency, failure in school, and sometimes suicide. It did not come as a surprise to me recently to read a report by an official in the Boy Scouts which stated that 40 percent of young adults between eighteen and twenty-two, and 31 percent of those between fifteen and seventeen feel they do not have a single friend that they can rely on. In the words of several who have experimented with drugs: "Drugs give me a warm feeling, a sort of substitute warm feeling that I would get from having a close friend." "Experimenting with drugs has put me in a new place; given me a new set of friends . . . even if they are drug-users."

The housewife experiences a similar situational type of loneliness. For one thing, her sources of love and attention are limited, being frequently confined to those within her home, and if her basic attention needs are not satisfied there, she will have no other outlets. Not so with the husband. Being out and about in the world, he has many more sources of attention. As the children grow and the housewife feels less needed by them, her more painful loneliness symptoms begin to emerge, driving her to cultivate friends away from the home setting—maybe even going out to work.

She also lives more of a role than the father. While he is frequently called by his first name by business friends and associates, she hears herself addressed as Mom, Mother, Mommy, Sweetie, Honey, and so on. She is constantly reminded of her role, and if she is conscientious she will probably do all she can to live up to it. But to live up to a role can be a lonely experience. In the process of expending all her energies in that direction, she may neglect or minimize her own personal interests, hobbies, wants, and needs. Unless she takes time to do some of the things that make her the unique *individual* that she is, she will gradually grow dead to them. But women tend to be more important in the eyes of the father and children for what they *do* rather than for what they *are*.

It is entirely predictable that if the parents have found it difficult to communicate down through the years, their individual fears of love are likely to be placed in sharp focus after the last child has left home. Up until that time preoccupation with the children helped them to avoid acknowledging the lack of communication and resulting loneliness in their own relationship. If both have been attempting to hide from their fear of love, it will now become obvious in some fashion. This, too, is situational loneliness because it is loneliness peculiar to this stage of their marriage.

If there has been an accumulation of unexpressed hurts and resentments they will probably come to the surface now. It can be a time of crisis. Each partner may decide to run even harder, with the wife finding shelter outside the home in a job. He, in turn, may arrange more of his appointments and meetings for the evening hours—a time when he is usually at home with his wife. The prospect of confrontation is too frightening. If the defenses centered on these fears have solidified, it is sometimes well-nigh impossible to penetrate them.

But the aged experience the deepest situational loneliness when they discover that they are sometimes simply forgotten or abandoned by their families. There are many fears expressed in the process of aging: fear of illness, loss of personal identity, independence, a job, or the death of a spouse. A relatively new term, retirement disease, describes what frequently happens during the first four months after retirement. It is then that there is a likelihood of heart attacks and strokes—all related to the trauma of a wide variety of losses.

In Chapter 10 the problem of age and loneliness is discussed in detail, for this sort of "situational loneliness" is a prospect each one of us must eventually face.

2 the walls people build around fear

I remember how my father responded to living things. One day in the woods I saw him slowly, almost lovingly, run his hand over the bark of a birch tree. Though I have forgotten his exact words, he said something about the beauty of its texture. I haven't seen anyone do anything like that since.

Loneliness is always related to the way in which we respond to people and to events. Sometimes it is with irritation, fear, guilt, sadness, and hurt; at other times it is with laughter and joy. This is particularly so with people about whom we care. It is not always understood that the opposite of love is not hate but indifference. The more we care about someone, the more positively we will react to them and what they are, do, and say.

Love and trust are not taught, they are caught. We parents do not teach our children to trust us by plunking them on our knees and saying, "I want you to trust me." As children observe the manner in which their parents trust each other, and as they themselves are trusted, so do they in turn learn to trust.

We will probably all agree that nothing living can survive on its own. A tree can exist only in relationship to the atmosphere, water, and soil. A fish lives only in relationship to the nutrients and life within the water. Similarly, a bird can exist only within the context of the trees, plants, and insects from which it gets sustenance. People also live and grow within the context of relationships.

In and of themselves, introspection and self-examination are dead-end streets. We grow through interaction with other people. They are continually bringing us to life through their understanding of us, their trust in us, and love for us; just as we in turn are doing the same for them.

Everyone, then, is born with influence. Even the tiny infant whose crying is slowly escalating into a nerve-shattering wail, is having a pronounced influence on other members of the family: toe-tapping, if not table-pounding, irritation. Others are always bringing out something in us. You have probably said of someone, "He brings out the worst in me." In all likelihood, you try to stay clear of that person. Being around him only causes unpleasant feelings inside you. But, on the other hand, you have undoubtedly said of others, "They bring out my best." In their presence your "good" feelings surface.

At bad times we mutter to ourselves, "Who needs people?" It is more than likely that these are the times when we feel the most afraid of love and so we have withdrawn, not only our physical body but also our trust. We are afraid to risk again.

Who needs people? It's like a tree saying, "Who needs the soil?" or a fish, "Who needs water?" In one way or another we *do* need people, but we *need* them for different reasons. The purpose for which we need them is related to the reason for which we need *strokes;* that need in turn being dependent upon our life position.

Strokes

When the doctor first gently slaps a newborn baby on the rump it may sting, but this is one time in the life of the child when a slap does something else. For someone who is but seconds old in a cold new world, that first touch, termed a stroke, also starts his will to live. Once "rescued," that initial stroke for the child also marks the inauguration of "stroking hunger," an ongoing need that, for his own growth or destruction, will have to be met.

Each of us, as it were, carries around a "stroke bucket," for strokes—if not one then probably two, one in each hand—looking for ways and means by which we might keep them filled.

Different strokes for different folks. Before we examine this statement in detail, let's list the different types of strokes:

Physical strokes. Our first strokes in life are physical ones—being held, rocked, or patted on the head. It is said that one of the reasons sailors love the sea is that the rocking and rolling motion brings to life feelings from childhood, the time they were rocked by their mothers. It felt good to be rocked. For many, the physical strokes are the kind that always feel the best, no matter how old they get.

Verbal strokes. Between the ages of one and three, the physical strokes are gradually replaced by verbal ones. Once again, because the child cannot intellectually understand the reason for the transfer, his root loneliness comes to the fore. Not understanding that he is becoming heavier to hold, especially when he squirms, he wonders: "What's happened? What is there about me *now* that is unlovable?"

Self strokes. There are several kinds, one being the good feelings that we experience after having exercised our own resources and used our hands and minds to create. For boys and men this might mean building a boat, cabinet, or tree-house; for girls and women, knitting a sweater, doing macramé, or baking something that others enjoy. Once we have finished we experience a feeling of worth and importance.

Other self strokes are of the desperate variety, sought by people when they are lonely to the point of panic. "There have been times when I felt so much in need of strokes and so lonely that I have even gone to the greeting-card rack in a drugstore and picked out and bought myself the sorts of cards I wish I were receiving from others. At one time I had quite a collection," one woman admitted with some reluctance. "On one occasion I remember even buying myself a corsage and wearing it. This was an occasion when I felt especially neglected and deprived by my husband. It was sort of a help because I felt I deserved the flowers, but lots of negative feelings went along with it, too. Like, here I was wearing these flowers and everyone thought they were a gift and how nice . . . but I knew better. The cards weren't so bad because I didn't try to deceive anyone with them except maybe myself. And then I didn't care about deceiving myself. I only wanted to feel better. I feel sort of silly about it now."

Another, living in a stroke vacuum, strokes herself by regularly clipping coupons from magazines and sending them in for the promised free samples and recipe booklets. This assures her of at least *some* mail from time to time and gives her something to look forward to. It is a stroke . . . but of the desperate variety.

Marshmallow strokes. These are airy nothings, compliments without substance, often given with more thought of a return than anything else. Some people are marshmallow champions, tossing compliments around like confetti at a wedding.

But marshmallow strokes can also be of the physical variety, gifts minus the heart of the giver. Halford Luccock writes of Dorcas, "a woman full of good works" who, in collecting clothing to send to Korea, reported that on several occasions women's coats came in with the buttons snipped off. Evidently the big-hearted givers felt the buttons were still good and cut them off for use on other garments, thus spoiling the gift. "The gift without the giver is bare," Luccock correctly observes.[1]

I am still having difficulty in forgiving the radio announcer who, before a recent Mother's Day, suggested: "Why not give Mother a set of tires on her big day?" Somehow that smacks of a marshmallow gift, to be verified with certainty if there is but one car in the family. But then again, I have since tried to give the announcer the benefit of the doubt, hoping that he meant, "only if Mother has her own car."

Conditional strokes. Meted out by the Parent, these strokes have strings attached to them: "I'll love you IF . . . you're good . . . do what Mommy says . . . the way I want it done . . . when I want it done." They are given only when performance meets *our* standards and values; no consideration or thought is given to the values of the other. For this reason, conditional strokers may be said to be engaging in blackmail.

Unconditional strokes. Given simply because we care, with no thought of a return, 100 percent gold in value.

Written strokes. In my desk there is a folder with the words *Stroke File* across the top. I refer to it as my stroke box because in it I have kept all kinds and types of letters, cards, and notes from my wife, children, and friends. When the strokes that I receive from outside sources are few (within the family, too), I will from time to time browse through the file and experience some of the good feelings that accompany such a review. After all, such strokes, even though I am reliving old ones, are better than none at all.

Vicarious strokes (also referred to as Western Union strokes). This is the giving and receiving of strokes through the medium of a third party; sometimes arranged with the third party directly, at other times with the "messenger" unwittingly manipulated. One woman, needing only to supplement her

[1] Halford Luccock, *Living Without Gloves* (New York: Oxford University Press, 1957), pp. 7–8.

second stroke bucket, arranged her own surprise birthday party with a cooperative friend. "How about it? If I pay the expenses, will you arrange it, telling people that it is going to be a surprise for me?" The party came off smoothly, with all the assembled guests enthusiastically crying, "Surprise, surprise!" when the birthday girl "just happened" to drop in at a prearranged location. She filled her auxiliary stroke bucket that night.

At other times it isn't just a matter of filling both buckets. If two people, lonely and afraid of love, do not stroke each other directly, either verbally or nonverbally, they may out of sheer desperation manipulate strokes through someone else. This Western Union method of stroke production was validated for me recently when a young housewife, lonely because her husband was afraid of love, spoke of the manner in which she has become skilled in using their six-year-old son to carry strokes back to her from her unsuspecting husband. She does this by sending the boy out to the garage or backyard, where her husband seems to spend most of his time. Sometimes she instructs the youngster to ask him a specific question and bring back his answer. At other times, he simply tags along behind his father, picking up bits and pieces of information that he in turn relays back to his mother. The husband rarely strokes her directly. Frequently he relates more of his ideas and feelings to their son than he does to her. Once again, the strokes she receives in this vicarious fashion are better than none at all. As long as the son cooperates, this arrangement may satisfy her attention needs. But when he tires of playing Western Union and his mother's stroke bucket is empty, there will be a crisis of some sort.

Some people discover that by virtue of their job, position, or role (particularly the wives of professional men and public officials), they are used as stroke messengers. Some may come to resent this after a time, but others thrive on it, because when they are depended upon and needed, this enables them to feel stroked also.

SCENE: A suburban high school the morning after the Spring Prom.

LINDA: Mary, I had a great time with Alex at the prom last night. Is there any way you can find out if he really likes me?

MARY: Let me hint around in the cafeteria at noon today, and I'll see you tonight after school in front of the gym.

In this case Mary may carry back a positive stroke to Linda. "He thinks you're terrific." But there is also the possibility that it could be a negative one, a clinker. "He just sort of grunted and walked away." Stroke bearers, toting negative strokes, can often become as depressed as the friends for whom they procure strokes, depending upon how negative the stroke is.

Ministers' wives are frequently the bearers of strokes, that responsibility being a part of the nonverbal contract at the time of marriage.

"Honey, did anyone say anything to you about my sermon this morning? No one said a word to me." If the stroke bucket she carries in his behalf is empty on that given Sunday afternoon, it could spark a depression in him (possibly in her, too), that extends through Sunday and into Monday, the severity of his depression coinciding with the number of hours he spent in preparing the sermon. On other Sundays, if she can risk it, she may bring back an occasional negative stroke, hoping against hope that it may work to his own benefit: "Martha told me that the sermon was a bit too long," or "Herb said that at one point you were too loud." His reaction will undoubtedly affect her willingness to share such criticism again in the future.

But on those days that she can figuratively tip out a full bucket of strokes on the kitchen table in front of him, he, and probably she, too, will have enough to carry them through *that* week and even into the following week. One positive stroke from a VIP can satisfy our stroking hunger for months.

Mailmen, the bearers of strokes in the form of letters, packages, and announcements of all types and kinds, are frequently met by people anxious for news from a son in the service, a note from a daughter at college, or a word from parents who are far away; birthday cards, wedding invitations, Christmas packages, and magazines—all are strokes, some with more value than others. Frequently, such appreciative people will meet the mailman at the door on a hot summer morning with a glass of lemonade; or on a blustery winter one with an invitation to have a cup of coffee.

Negative strokes. These, discussed below, are the type needed, and sought after, when we feel unlovable. Since they are of the "kick me" variety, they do what they are intended to do—confirm for us our Not OK-ness.

Circus strokes. These are procured by sensational dress or behavior: women smoking cigars at a public gathering, men carrying purses, wearing unusual jewelry, flashing $100 bills in public, children intentionally burping at mealtime (both circus and negative, but it does get them the attention that they want and need), profanity and vulgarity in circles where they are frowned on.

Stroke addicts are those who never seem to be able to fill their buckets, the most probable reason being that in our Not OK-ness, we are always downgrading the strokes that we do receive.

I sometimes give my clients what I call a stroke list. On a sheet of paper they are asked to write down the names of people to whom they can go to give strokes and to get them. "But isn't that awfully superficial?" some people ask. In my opinion it is not. While we would all like to live in situations where stroking is spontaneous, at times when it is not forthcoming we simply have to go after it.

Dr. Thomas A. Harris, in giving a clue as to the value of

strokes, said, "When in doubt, always stroke." One of the most positive strokes that we can give is to call acquaintances by their first names. To meet someone again whom you met only once, ten or fifteen years before, and to have him remember you after that lapse of time by your first name is a stroke that is unparalleled. While it may feed the ego of professionals to be called Doctor, Judge, and so forth, I often have the feeling that most would like nothing better than to risk saying, "Let's drop the title . . . how about calling me by my first name?"

The three walls

We are lonely because we build walls instead of bridges.

I'M NOT OK—YOU'RE OK. "I'm not lovable . . . and I'll prove it." While the child expresses anger, hurt, sadness, joy, or laughter, the most potent and overriding emotion that he experiences is fear. It overshadows all the others. Though with increasing awareness and understanding we can turn down the volume on that fear, there is no way of guaranteeing that it can be turned off permanently. Our hope, however, lies in the fact that we will be able gradually to turn down the volume with our Adult.

In this universal position, there is a *need* to prove that we are unlovable. And so we unconsciously manipulate others in order that they will reinforce for us our own fears of love. There is, as it were, in our Not OK Child, a very elaborate *stroke recycling machine* that is designed to intercept positive strokes and to recycle them in such a manner that what comes out as the finished product are negative strokes. The machine is in operation from sunup to sundown, manned by two shifts —each eight hours in duration—with no graveyard shift because that is when we are sleeping.

It works like this: When a 100 percent gold compliment is given, no matter for what reason, it is intercepted first by

the Not OK in our Child and immediately fed into the recycling machine, so that a "Harry, I appreciate the fine job
you've done over the past couple of months" stroke emerges
at the opposite end of the machine as a negative one—"Oh,
anybody could have done it." Because the machine is designed to either downgrade or minimize the value of strokes
(because this is something the Not OK Child has to do),
and yes, sometimes even reject them, the label on the finished
product reads: "I'm really nothing." The machine then is
designed for the purpose of continually reaffirming our self
worth: I'M NOT LOVABLE.

"I'd really like to get to know you better," when recycled
will come out, "If he really knew what I was like he wouldn't
say that." The label: I'M NOT LOVABLE.

If our Not OK Child is not busy recycling incoming *positive*
strokes, then it is busy manipulating others directly for *negative*
ones. Do any of these sound familiar to you?

I'm always wrong.
I haven't gotten a thing done.
I know I can't.
You always win.
You're smarter than I am.
You're always right.
You always get your way.
You're so efficient.
You get things done.
You're so organized.

The "kicks" come back to us in this form:

What's wrong with you anyway?
I can't stand your lousy attitude.
Do you think you could ever handle success?
How come you're so negative?

We win by losing. The kicks that we get serve to keep our fears
alive, and our self image negative. To win would be frighten-

ing. We simply wouldn't know how to handle any good feelings about ourselves.

In this life position, then, *positive strokes do not register;* they don't get a chance. This brings us to another important thing to remember about strokes. *All the stroking in the world will not make us feel more OK until we have taken that basic position with ourselves.* A case in point is the distraught and bewildered husband, a good stroker by nature, who said to his wife, "You certainly seem to thrive on my pity, but why is it that you can't accept the compliments that I want to give to you?" She *needed* his pity and kicks (negative strokes) in order that he might reaffirm for her, "I'm unlovable." Not only was she a frightened and lonely woman, but in addition she was nudging her husband into a similar position. He, too, was lonely because although he wanted to give of himself she was unable to accept. He was being robbed of the joy of giving, becoming more and more reluctant (and afraid) to give what he wanted to give. Both of them were lonely.

In a desperate attempt to cope with overwhelming fears of "I'm unlovable," we may build a second wall and take on the reverse position of I'M OK—YOU'RE NOT OK. "I don't trust anyone who might want to show that they care about me." ("What's behind the strokes?") People frequently assume this position as a means of self-preservation. If our feelings of being unlovable become unbearable (with accompanying loneliness), in a desperate effort to block them out we will switch to an angry position of "If it weren't for the world." As long as we can blame what's "out there" we don't have to experience our own loneliness pain. People in this position give the appearance of sureness, arrogance, and snobbery, but it is a posture devised to keep others at a distance, trusting no one, not least of all those who want to *give love.* Beneath the sneers, insults, anger, and belligerence, however, is an agonizing fear of love.

Of all the feelings in our arsenal, anger is the most predictable one. We can be reasonably sure of how someone will react if we become angry; they will in all likelihood become angry too. Because we know this *in advance*, at the point in communication where we are reacting with increasing hurt or feelings of rejection and fear, we will sometimes become angry. It is a way of shutting down the dialogue and the possibility of further shattered feelings. On occasion we all use anger as a defensive weapon, but others whose fear of love has become unbearable will freeze into this position. They can no longer bear to cope with their fear of love. This life-style allows them to *win*, which they must do at all costs, even if it means resorting to homicide. But their win is only temporary. In the end they always lose because the other is continually being placed in the position of being wrong, and "blamed" for everything. That breeds estrangement and loneliness.

The bully never allows others to know what he is thinking or feeling. The anger that he projects masks all his inner feelings, particularly his fear. In that sense he always remains a stranger to us. We may probe and ask questions but it is always to no avail. This is the most difficult of walls to penetrate. People who use power as a means of controlling others are among the loneliest people of all, although they would never admit it. The angrier they get, the lonelier they are because people become increasingly afraid of them. At the point when such a person can admit to his fear of love (I'M NOT OK) he will have taken the first step in the direction of cure. Until that time all of his energy will be spent in using power and control in an effort to prove to himself and others that he is OK (MORE OK).

But there is also a third wall, a wall of despair: I'M NOT OK—YOU'RE NOT OK. It is the "surrender" position; an inability to either give or take strokes. The fear of loving has degener-ated into paralysis. There is utter black loneliness.

In assuming the I'M OK—YOU'RE OK position we begin

to move away from the position of simply reacting to the position of responsible acting. Before we can say that others are OK, however, we must arrive at that decision about our own worth. In infancy our estimate as to our self worth was a conclusion based on *feelings alone*. Now it is a *choice* based on a storehouse of data.

The OK position is not a port that we arrive at and where we permanently anchor, but rather a road that we are always traveling, inching ahead and then slipping back, but gaining a bit each time, FEELING MORE OK. The struggle goes on for a lifetime and our attitude as to the worth of that struggle determines the degree of our loneliness.

3 how we escape responsibility for our loneliness

There are many myths about loneliness. Some are the direct result of unawareness as to its nature, but the majority are an attempt to escape the responsibility for our fear of love. Most of the loneliness that we feel is of our own doing. The conclusions we arrived at as little persons were based on our unawareness. In a sense we were victims then, having only the ability to *react*. But it is possible to continue through life in much the same fashion.

To illustrate: The most popular games of childhood are "If it weren't for you," "See what you made me do," and "It's all your fault"; all games that place the responsibility for hurt, fear, or mistakes "out there." Blaming others for our hurts enables us to do something about them. We always have to do something. A child does everything except the helpful things as a means of dealing with a pain that he does not intellectually understand. Out of his unawareness (a yet tottering and sometimes lurching inner Adult), he will deal with it the only way he knows how: blaming big people for everything from the milk he knocks over with his elbow ("If YOU hadn't put my glass so near the edge of the table") and his stomach aches ("Mother, if YOU hadn't made me eat that ickey corn"), to his fear of love ("Why are YOU always so mean to me?").

Eric Berne's *Games People Play*[1] failed to note that man's first and favorite game, "If it weren't for you," was originally played at the time of creation. Such irresponsibility is as old as time itself. In the biblical story of Adam and Eve, God told the pair that they were not to eat of one tree in the garden, the "tree of knowledge." But because of the same compulsion that prompts little boys to strike the matches they are told not to strike, and little girls to touch hot burners on the stove they are told not to touch, so it was with Eve. Her curiosity won; she picked what she was instructed not to pick. And because misery loves company she then proceeded to involve Adam. "Here, have some." When God, in the wake of this, asked Eve what had happened, she promptly proceeded to blame the snake that tempted her. "*He* made me do it." When Adam in turn was queried by God, he fired back a double-barreled broadside: "*You* gave her to me and *she* made me do it." Double irresponsibility. Both did their best to wriggle out of the consequences of a choice that they had made as individuals—"We're victims."

It seemed to come as naturally to them as it does to us now. When comedian Flip Wilson cracks, "The devil made me do it," it rings bells for all of us. Blaming others for our hurts, fears, mistakes, poor judgment, and misfortunes enables us as big people to do something about them. The only difference is that the forty-year-old's excuse is probably more sophisticated than the five-year-old's. We may be able to justify our bitterness and fear by playing the role of victim—"See what you made me do." Big people who still insist on playing victim, however, are living out the very same role that they played as helpless children.

[1] Eric Berne, *Games People Play* (New York: Grove Press, 1964).

Victims

As victims, therefore, we are unwilling to take the responsibility for our *decisions, feelings,* and *behavior.* The prospect is frightening. We are forever mumbling, "If it weren't for them . . . you . . . her . . . him." But behind this theme song there is a fear of accepting personal responsibility for our *decisions.* We always leave a tiny escape hatch through which we can duck if things turn sour. We are not willing to give a firm and resounding yes or no to anything or anyone. Characterized by such half-hearted statements as "I'll try," "maybe," "I suppose," and "I hope so," we will do anything to avoid having to make a definite commitment.

In playing victim we are also afraid of our own feelings, responding only with feelings that are in keeping with what people expect and want us to feel, but frequently denying what really lies inside us—anger, hurt, sadness, fear, even joy. Allowing ourselves to be constantly hurt, we roll over and play dead when it comes to doing something about our hurts. In nursing wounds for days, months, or years, we set up what is called a *feeling racket;* hurt or anger that we have no intention of doing a thing about, which allows us to feel what we need to feel—always rejected, hurt, or afraid.

"Why don't you?" "Yes, but," is a favorite feeling racket (and game) of the lonely person. Though he will often solicit advice from his doctor, minister, or some other professional, which on the surface seems to be Adult in nature, wondering how he can rise above a particular hurt, he gingerly responds to each suggestion or option with "Yes, but," a game that proceeds through four stages.

HOOK

"Doctor, I have this problem. Sherry used to call me all the time . . . and we used to get together, but she's stopped calling. What is there about me, anyway?" (Adult.)

MANEUVER

A lively discussion centered on possible options: "Why don't you . . . ?" (Still Adult.)

GIMMICK

"Yes, but, I have tried what you suggest. This didn't seem to work because—" or "That just didn't seem possible." Probably the grand champion response is, "You just don't seem to understand me." This sudden switch from Adult to Child happens because the "victim" verbalizes what her inner Not OK Child was up to all along; a need to place the responsibility on someone else for her feelings of being unlovable, in this case her doctor.

PAYOFF

She will be able to collect another hurt. In addition to feeling unlovable to her neighbors and friends she can now claim that her doctor didn't even care enough about her to muster up the understanding that she was looking for: "Even *he* doesn't understand me." She can now continue with her racket.

When it comes to thinking of new and unique excuses for not implementing a suggested solution or option, the hardcore, go-for-broke "Why don't you?" "Yes, but" player may approach something bordering on sheer genius. But the harder she plays "Yes, but" the lonelier she becomes.

How to begin: the ladder of risk

Once we are sure that we want to throw our feeling racket overboard, it is best to begin by taking *small risks* at first; risks with our feelings and choices. If we begin with big ones, and if things go wrong, we may not be able to assume responsibility for the painful reaction. We begin much in the fashion of a swimmer who tests the temperature of the ocean by putting his big toe in the water; then wading in up to his ankles, waist, shoulders, all the while taking the time to allow his body to adjust to the temperature change. So with our loneliness. If we begin with small risks and the response is one to which we react with hurt ("Here we go again!"), it is easier for us to regroup our inner forces.

Jim, a beleaguered, lonely husband, had the right idea. He began by deciding that he would call his wife on the telephone from work every noon. Sick of his "I'm not lovable" racket, and having been in an I'M NOT OK—YOU'RE OK position with his wife for many years, he had *allowed* himself to be hurt by almost everything she said, only rarely risking an expression of his personal feelings in return. When he became aware of the way in which he had been merely reacting to her, he decided that the safest and most responsible way to begin to trust his feelings again would be to talk to her over the telephone.

One reason we are frightened at the prospect of sharing our feelings is that any negative (imagined or real) expression on the face of the listener is more often than not interpreted as disgust, disapproval, misunderstanding, or rejection. These physical reactions may well ignite our fears again and we withdraw. Jim knew that initially he would be on the lookout (as he always had been) for any such negative expression on her face. But once he discovered that his wife was willing to listen over the telephone, he took the next step by writing his feelings down on paper. Once again he would not have to talk to her face to face, but at least he was expressing his feelings, and in the process slowly learning to trust them again. As often as possible he allowed the words to flow from his pen, not rehearsing in advance what he was going to write. Rehearsing what we are going to express can easily stifle a free flow of feeling.

Fearing that it won't look acceptable, or sound right, we rehearse. In Jim's case, he felt that his wife was more intel-

ligent than he was anyway. It was a real victory for him to rise
above his fear of not coming across in an intelligent manner to
her and simply allowing words to flow from his pen. At first
he tore the notes up. Still fighting a fear of being misunderstood, he could not risk the anticipated reaction. ("If she
really gets to know what I'm like, she is certain not to like
me.") But in time he began to give them to her. Lo and behold,
once again she understood. Ironically, it was what she had
always hoped for, so she was more than delighted. When he
discovered that she not only accepted the full range of his
feelings but was delighted that he no longer felt like a
stranger to her, his own fear of love began to dissipate, to
thaw. He is now beginning to talk about his feelings to her
directly. Having slowly worked his way up the ladder of risk,
he is in the position of being more responsible for all of his
feelings; trusting them more and consequently being less
afraid of love.

When we first begin to take small risks, *initiative* is the
key word; taking the initiative and greeting a stranger before
he speaks, taking the risk of inviting a new (or old) neighbor
over for coffee some morning, taking the risk of instigating
a conversation with someone sitting in the seat next to you on
the bus, train, or plane. One lonely man decided that the
first real risk he would take would be to say "Hello" to every
stranger at a convention that he was about to attend. He came
back elated. No one stared at him in numbed silence (which
was part of the risk he took); everyone said something to him
in return.

There is no guarantee that little risks will not backfire either.
"If I am a little lonely, I can call a friend on the phone,"
someone says. "But here there is risk, too. Perhaps the
friend hasn't the time to chat or is not in a good mood. If
I am only a little lonely then I can accept this and feel better
for having made the effort and even switch to feeling sympathy
for the friend's problem. In the same vein I can take a small

risk by cheering someone else up; can visit an elderly person or someone else who may be lonely."

How risks may upset the balance of relationships

When lonely, frightened people first begin to take small risks with their feelings and decisions they can sometimes upset the balance of their relationships. Wives, husbands, business associates, children, and friends are apt to be not only bewildered but also belligerent. Having never seen this side of the person before, the change can have a dire effect on their own security and role.

To see someone change from a frog (Eric Berne's description of a loser) into a prince or princess does not always prompt people to applaud. Human nature being what it is, change in others can threaten us.

"Just who does Al think he is," the boss, red-necked, is apt to say, "telling me he resents having to work overtime? He always has before, at no extra pay." Or: "Margaret has always gone along with my suggestions and ideas. I just don't understand what has come over her. . . . She's getting so independent."

Adjustment will have to be made on both sides. A person who is just beginning to trust his own feelings and decision-making machinery, unless understood by others, will regress. Conversely, he will have to understand that this previously unexpressed side of him (a side that has been alien to him because it has always been his "bad" side) may bewilder, frighten, threaten, and anger those who surround him in his everyday life.

The point is, we do not have to be victims. Once we become aware that we are responsible for the nature of our choices and the manner in which we handle our feelings, we begin to grow up. But even more important, our loneliness thaws.

In the final analysis, nothing lasting is ours through luck, chance, or accident. To wait for a lucky break is irresponsibility at its height. If we have failed, it is because we lacked the ability, skill, judgment, energy, interest, or willingness to take risks for the one specific thing we set out to do. To feel that life has cheated us, that others were unfair or cruel, or that someone didn't support us who should have done so is to place the blame on them for our miserable lot in life.

It isn't what happens to us, it is how we choose to *react* to what happens to us. We cannot always control such matters as the illnesses that strike us down, the close friends who move away, the layoffs from work, the loss of a relative or mate through death, or loss of property through flood or tornado. But we do have a choice in determining how we are going to react, on an ongoing basis, to these events. Sometimes people do not treat us fairly or with much consideration. At those times we feel let down and are apt to feel rejected. But rarely do people do things deliberately to hurt or reject us. Our Not OK-ness has a *need* to "read in" rejection. It is our choice. If others are tired, irritated (often at someone other than us), are feeling physically worn out or even afraid of love themselves, the natural tendency for us is to assume that their indifference or lack of response is willful rejection of us. Again, "I'm unlovable."

"Yes," you say, "but others do hurt me." No one can deny that others hurt us. What they say about us and to us can hurt us badly sometimes. But happily we have a choice in how we are going to deal with our initial hurt feelings *after* we become aware of having experienced them. Our first response to what someone has said or done flows from deep down within us. We have no control over it. But once we become aware of our response (Adult), we are *responsible* for the manner in which we are going to handle it from that moment on. In other words, *we have a choice.*

One option is to go inward with our hurt, to withdraw and

brood, for days, even months or years. By withdrawing we become more afraid of love because of our certainty that if we love again, we will be hurt again.

We may attempt to block out our hurt by plunging into an endless round of activities, or by drinking or taking drugs. We place ourselves in the center of the action in order to try to forget. But unexpressed feelings don't just go away. They become unfinished business for the future. We can become, as Dr. William Glasser puts it, "historians," keeping a ledger of unexpressed hurts or "mads."

We may deal with our feelings in an outward manner when they are felt; simply stating our immediate reaction without in any way attempting to make others responsible for our reaction. In other words, we can risk—but with some semblance of responsibility.

Risk is to understanding and love what a wick is to a candle, its very center. Such risking gives us an opportunity to experience ourselves more fully. Besides, it allows the other to see if our reaction coincided with his intent. In the process we are becoming better acquainted.

But do others always want to know of our reactions? Casual acquaintances could probably not care less. Besides, it would serve no good purpose. Much to our dismay though, we may also find that members of our immediate families do not always want to know of our reactions either. If friends and intimates spurn them, then obviously they are not interested in knowing us.

There are situations in which it is not wise to share our reactions with others. If your boss has said or done something to which you reacted with anger, to say, "I'm annoyed with you," might place your job in jeopardy. That kind of risk isn't worth it. Then it is the better part of wisdom to look for other ways to release anger. Some men do this by whacking away at a golf ball, engaging in a vigorous game of tennis or handball, or even throwing stones against a fence. "I do my very best housework," explains a wife who works part time, "when I am angry at my boss." Anger, if it is to dissipate, must be dealt with by action. A set of drums for a boy, though the noise may drive his parents up the wall, provides a fine outlet for anger. Even target shooting gives a type of release. Hearing the report of the gun does something to help dissipate anger.

Several of the myths about loneliness will no doubt sound familiar to you.

1. "It's impossible to experience loneliness as long as I am with people."

It is possible to feel more alone in a crowd than on a mountaintop. If we are afraid of love, the presence of other people, even the contemplation of times when we will be with them, may serve to intensify our fears, making us even more lonely.

Whenever I teach a course on Loneliness at one of our local colleges several persons will initiate a dialogue with me beforehand. The conversation follows a predictable pattern and goes like this:

Mr. B. "Say, I see that you're starting another series on Loneliness at the college?"

I. T. "Right. Our first class begins in two weeks. Interested?"

Mr. B. "You know, I'm so involved with people in civic and church affairs that being lonely is the *one thing I am not.*"

In the same fashion in which we live with the delusion that broken limbs, ghastly car accidents, and sudden death happen to others but never to us, so it is with loneliness. It is something that happens to other people; so goes the myth.

But central to our examination of loneliness is the firm belief that a crammed schedule of community commitments on the kitchen calendar is no guarantee that involvement alone gives us an immunity to the disease. If anything, the opposite is true. One of the basic reasons for our accelerated pace of life today is that we are *running* from loneliness. Never have people been more active outside the home than they are today;

yet never have more individuals exhibited more of the symptoms of loneliness. The question is, Are we running *to* or *from*
something? I say it is the latter.

If you have been in a large city alone, you probably know
what it's like to brush elbows with dozens of strangers, look
briefly into their eyes with a momentary feeling that "Maybe
we could be friends," but then with an overwhelming feeling
of distrust and fear. It isn't accidental that well-known per-
sonalities commit suicide. Many of them, being afraid of love
(people find this hard to believe), discover that becoming
popular, having one's name up in lights, means being pushed
suddenly into the limelight and surrounded by admiring, ag-
gressive crowds. As a result, their already present fear of love
is aggravated to the point of despair, panic and, ultimately,
suicide. Its pain becomes too much to bear.

Loneliness has to do, not with the number of friends who
surround us, but with the quality of our friendship. *One
understanding friend will fulfill a need in us that a milling,
swirling crowd of a thousand cannot.*

2. "I never choose to be lonely." Another myth. Some persons, because of their fears of love, will sometimes keep themselves at a distance from us. We may try to win them over,
but to no avail. We should not conclude automatically that
there is something about *us* that is unlovable. Their fear
of love is something they must handle and for which they are
responsible. This does not mean that we ignore them, but
rather, if possible, let them know that we would *like* to understand them. It is such understanding that may eventually result
in their coming out from behind their protective walls. If we
judge them, it will only serve to widen the gulf between us.

3. "It is important to work hard at not being lonely." If that
means working hard to be popular, to be the constant center
of attention, or to be loved by everyone, then it is a very
exhausting business. Fear lies behind our frantic efforts to make
ourselves lovable to everyone.

4. "Only a few people ever seem to do anything about their

loneliness." *In one way or another, everyone does something about his loneliness pain.* It is just too miserable a feeling to leave untreated. If we do not exercise the positive alternatives to it with some understanding, then out of our ignorance and unawareness we will unconsciously continue to employ the techniques of manipulation that we have utilized since the time we were children, the only difference being that, as big people, those techniques will probably be more subtle. *Discounting* is one such destructive method. Discounting of people requires a great deal of shrewd maneuvering and planning, particularly if we know in advance of those times when circumstances are going to place us in the same place at the same time—church on Sunday morning, the annual company Christmas party, or a PTA meeting. What is disconcerting for the discounter are those unexpected moments of actual confrontation. There is no panic that quite equals that of a woman suddenly spotting "that person" in a supermarket, rounding the corner at the far end of the aisle, slowly pushing her grocery cart in her direction. But hard-core discounters will find a way of avoiding physical confrontation, even if it means testing the firmness of twenty-five heads of lettuce in the vegetable section rather than the usual two or three. For reasons such as this, and because discounting requires more than just a minimum expenditure of energy, discounters discover that they are in various stages of emotional exhaustion. This in turn means that they have little energy left with which to care genuinely about people.

We also resort to *gossip* as a means of equalizing our loneliness pain. It is always about individuals who have hurt us. One popular technique is to raise seemingly innocent questions about their character. Rather than blatantly and openly assaulting someone's character, we ask "innocent" questions about it. It is enough to leave a question of doubt in the minds of our listeners: "Is it true that . . . ?" "I have heard that . . ." "Do you suppose that . . . ?"

5. "There is a connection between loneliness and my sur-

roundings." Our loneliness is not related to the place where we live, whether urban or rural, or to the caliber of our friends, neighbors, and associates. The solution to our loneliness would be an easy matter if it meant merely picking up stakes and moving to a friendlier neighborhood or getting a new job. Neighbors who do not respond to our friendly overtures may make us angry and more afraid of love. But wherever we go there will always be those who do not respond to our loving. A change of environment may give us temporary relief and excitement, but if things go badly again—and there is no guarantee that they will not—it can easily degenerate into a never-ending cycle of restlessness and moving, living in the delusion that it will always be better somewhere else. Manipulation of our environment is no lasting solution to loneliness. Once again, that places the responsibility for our feelings of loneliness out there, away from ourselves; putting it on the town, neighborhood, job, culture, school, politics, church, minister, and so on. There is no way we can justify or defend our fears of love and loneliness. We are always responsible.

Boredom is commonly mistaken for loneliness; people in rural areas especially are apt to link the two. "It sure is lonely way out here in the boondocks," complained a serviceman whose tour of duty placed him in a remote military installation that was nothing more than a clearing hacked out of a sea of cactus. In his case, he was not lonely but bored, not knowing how to pass the time during his free hours. Again, loneliness is always equated with a fear of love. This serviceman will simply, difficult though it may be, have to work at new ways of passing time.

Sometimes, however, boredom is the direct result of loneliness. If, afraid of love, we withdraw, the problem becomes: Now how do I pass the time? Several people have told me that even though they are ill at ease with people, they enjoy watching them; sitting on a bench in the park watching a spinster feed the pigeons, a whistling kid shining shoes, two lovers on another bench, an eccentric old gentleman parading in all sincerity with a homemade cardboard sign reading *Repent Now. The End Is Near.* Watching people may not be very rewarding in terms of fulfilling our need for love, but it does provide us with an outlet to avoid becoming bored. Boredom, then, may be linked to loneliness, but only if our boredom is the result of withdrawal from people because we are afraid of love.

6. "Loneliness and aloneness are the same thing." This is our most common and misleading myth. *It is possible to be alone and not be lonely.* Some people are loners by choice, choosing aloneness as a life-style. The fur trapper out in the wilds, the forest ranger, prospector, lighthouse keeper, rancher, and farmer are usually loners, and never seem to complain about being lonely. But aside from these people, aloneness also has to do with *feelings of loss* following a *physical* separation from familiar and loved places and people. It is at such times that our aloneness is keenly experienced, especially if we did not choose the separation.

All of us at one time or another have *chosen* to separate ourselves from job, friends, family, in order to think, reflect, and evaluate in the quietness of a place apart. This I have done on a number of occasions by retreating to our summer cabin. Whether I have been chopping wood, hiking, or sitting by the lake chewing on a blade of grass, it has been good to experience what happens in isolation. It is painful sometimes, but nevertheless good. After a few days I have often become restless and returned home again to my family. We need to be alone, but we also need intimacy and understanding with and from others. There is a time and place for both.

But when our separation physically from others has not been by choice but through the natural flow of events, our sudden aloneness can leave us numb and in painful despair. This is especially so when we have been separated from loved ones through death. It can happen in a split second. Billy Graham reminds us that "Everyone is but one heartbeat away from death . . . no matter how healthy he is." This is not meant to be grim in tone, but is a reality and is something that we easily forget. Separation from loved ones through death can come at the most unexpected moments. We do not *choose* separation this way. There are separations over which we may grieve for years. At other times we are better able to accept them. When that happens we use resources within ourselves that we had either lost contact with or had never tapped, new discoveries and appreciations.

The word aloneness refers to the feeling of loss in the aftermath of a physical separation from that which is familiar and loved, whether people, places, or pets. An old bachelor, grieving over a dog that had been his companion for fifteen years, put it this way: "That dog was my *whole* life." He was not only saying that he missed his dog, but that the reality of his aloneness now was most painful and vivid.

Loneliness is totally different. It is not separation from people in a physical sense but separation from them emotionally. It is being close physically, but feeling distant emotionally . . . because of our fear of love.

7. "I feel loneliest at particular times of the year." It is easy to confuse loneliness with feelings of nostalgia or melancholy. Our moments of nostalgia usually coincide with certain seasons of the year: anniversaries, birthdays, holidays, occasions and events that result in a replay of good or sad feelings out of the past.

The smell of leaves burning in the fall or fresh home-baked bread may provoke nostalgia, as may the sight of a beautiful sunset on a warm summer night. Even sounds—the wind rustling the leaves of a willow tree or the chatter of crickets outside our bedroom window at night—can provoke melancholy. In our aloneness at such moments we may miss the physical presence of someone with whom we previously shared such quiet and tender times. In an effort to experience our nostalgia fully we may choose to withdraw for a time, even allowing ourselves to cry. While some of our nostalgia is equated with loved ones no longer with us, at other times it has to do with places and incidents where, by ourselves, we were deeply stirred by beauty or tragedy. But to reaffirm what has been said, loneliness is *always* equated with a fear of love. In our nostalgia we may sometimes say that we are lonely, but it is nostalgia and should not be confused with loneliness.

Having more than one basket

"Placing all our eggs in one basket" means that we look to one person as the supplier of all our attention needs. While this may, for a while, be flattering to the other, it is more than likely that eventually the load of such responsibility will become heavy, heavy even to the point of resentment. Lonely people, whose fear of love will not allow them to risk much with many, are apt to have but one "basket"; it is safer that way. But this decision will be disastrous if and when that one source of attention moves away or dies. At that point we will have no one else to turn to. For that reason it is good to have a number of friends.

We do not care for two individuals in exactly the same manner. This makes it possible for us to care for two, three, or ten people all at the same time. The love that we feel for our mates is different from the love that we feel for our children. Sometimes we may feel guilty in saying "I love you" to a friend. It's almost as if we are being unfaithful and disloyal to wives, husbands, and children, a type of betrayal. I would like to suggest that we never love our friends in the same manner with which we love our mates. This is not an affront to either; it is a compliment. What we are saying is that we love each in keeping with our belief that no two people are alike.

Have ten wants

When lonely we are apt to place everybody else's wants first and ours a poor last. When we do this, it is more than likely we will lose touch with our wants. For this reason I often ask my patients to list, in order of preference, ten things that their inner Natural Child wants the most that day. If we feel unlovable we are probably investing a greater amount of our energy into making ourselves lovable—overcompensating, overpromising, overworking—which in turn usually results in overdrinking, oversmoking, and overeating. Such self-deprivation is easily rationalized as "sacrifice," classified as noble, exemplifying the humble servant. In our loneliness it is difficult for us to determine the line at which sacrifice degenerates into "I don't deserve it," or martyrdom.

A want list for a woman may include anything at all. For instance, here are ten wants:

1. Be less afraid of my feelings
2. Do more entertaining with my husband
3. Get out of debt within two years
4. Write a short story
5. Go around the world with my husband within the next ten years
6. Work at having more friends
7. Give strokes and get more strokes
8. Get my weight down to 120 pounds
9. Attend a night class in sewing
10. Learn to fly an airplane

After an individual has listed her wants, she is asked to take the first item on her list and carefully evaluate the way she is going to proceed toward the fulfillment of it.

1. Who and why—Evaluate who wants it, the Parent, Adult, or Child, and why each wants it.

2. Data—How much will it cost? Whom will this involve? Answer as many information questions as you can about this want.

3. Price—What price must your Parent, Adult, and Child pay? If your Child gets this want, will your Adult be strong enough to keep your Parent from "beating on your inner

Child"? If your Parent wants to save for something big, will the Child pay the price for doing without those little things that make the Child happy?

4. Options—This entry extends the items in your want list. By this time, after gathering data, you might be aware of many more options for reaching this want. Also, you should evaluate each of these options and how they affect the prices being paid.

5. Start/Stop Time—When are you going to start and stop working on this want? When do you plan to reach this want? How will this data affect the prices being paid?

6. Rewards—What are some of the side benefits you will get besides getting this specific want?[2]

	Parent	Adult	Child
Want			
Data			
Price			
Options			
Start/Stop			
Rewards			

We all have wants that are unique to each of us. No two people have the same wants. Even if they are dreams, they are wants. The persistence with which we pursue our dreams is sometimes an indication of how much worth we place upon ourselves.

[2] Want List data compiled by Dr. Thomas A. Harris and associates.

4 to feel understood
is to feel loved

Whom do you feel important to today? With a high degree of accuracy it can be said that we feel important to the people who "work" to understand us. There's something to this: to feel understood is to feel loved.

"All I ask is that you understand how I feel." On the face of things that doesn't seem to be asking for too much. But understanding is the most *costly* gift that someone can give us. Obviously the cost is not in money or things but in giving themselves. In relation to others, the opposite of loneliness is understanding. Nothing thaws loneliness more quickly than understanding. Such occasions are of short duration. Whether it is for one minute, ten minutes, or an hour, at such moments we stand on the other side of loneliness. If the frequency and duration of those times are becoming longer, however, it means that we are gradually moving off dead center.

To the consternation of more than just a few, love between two people is not characterized by total agreement or similarity of life-style. We don't always stubbornly insist that those who are the closest to us nod their heads in agreement with everything that we say. To be able to disagree but yet communicate the message that we understand the other person is the basis for a healthy relationship. In the process of seeking understanding from someone, three necessary things happen:

1. We give to another the gift of ourselves. "Daddy, what did you bring me this time?" our four-year-old Mary Beth asked breathlessly on my return from a brief trip. "Honey," I responded with a little trepidation, "this time I didn't bring you candy bars or a toy . . . just *me*." With that she stomped off in the direction of her room. The gift of "me" isn't always appreciated, accepted, or understood for what it is. Understandably, kids sometimes have a hard time choosing between chocolate bars and people, between things and human beings. But so do adults, only on a more sophisticated level . . . and for different reasons.

We can give nothing more personal of ourselves to someone else than our feelings and fantasies. To give ourselves means to give what is *alive in us at the moment,* our ideas, opinions, likes, dislikes, preferences, wishes, dreams, fantasies (which are the most frightening things of all to share, because people may think of us as weird), and also to express sadness, hurt, fear, anger, joy, laughter, or to touch. Next to fantasies, the most personal thing about each of us is our feelings. The thoughts and ideas that we share are often subject to judgment and misunderstanding, and the prospect of such a reaction will sometimes make us hesitant to share them. But there is an even greater reluctance to *give* our feelings. To share them is to share the most personal component of our person. Feelings lie at the core of our being. Nothing about us is more personal, more delicate. They comprise what is termed our inner Natural Child, the part of us that, in addition, appreciates beauty in nature and in people. But it is also the part of us that can be the most easily hurt. And so we will not want to share our feelings with just anyone. We are selective, choosing carefully the people we will "risk" with.

One distraught housewife, in pleading for understanding from her defensive husband, cried: "The anger, hurt, fear, sadness, or joy that I give to you is simply *my way* of reacting to you at the moment." She was pleading that *her way* be understood and accepted. Our immediate reaction to others is not good or bad, right or wrong. It is simply *our* reaction, for better or for worse. In expressing reactions we are allowing others to know us. If we withhold them (particularly with people about whom we care) then we will remain strangers to each other. Our intention in giving them is not to hurt others, although this will sometimes happen. Instead, we give in the hope that our reactions will be understood. Once we feel understood then we will willingly proceed into a deeper dialogue centering on the nature of our reactions.

No two people react to an event with the same quality or intensity of feeling. This may lead either to resentment or to excitement in a relationship. It will lead to the latter if there is an interest and curiosity in knowing how the other reacted, but it will lead to resentment if there is a belief that the different reactions and disagreement imply a lack of love. *An appreciation of dissimilarity is vital in a relationship that is characterized by understanding.* When we give our reaction, it is with the hope that others will recognize and value the uniqueness of our gift. If they detract from it by measuring it by the standpoint of their own experience, or if it is compared with the reaction of others, then they have not accepted us for what we are at that moment. It is at such moments that we make decisions as to whether or not such sharing is worthwhile. Out of fear we may decide that it would be safer in the future to substitute things rather than to give of ourselves —not our anguish or joy, our ideas, opinions, or anger, but chocolates, clothes, and other presents. But we may also turn to children or pets. A female patient commented: "When I am especially afraid of adults, I might seek out a little child and play with him. Little ones do not often reject me. Or perhaps I will go to a pet, a dog or a cat, and talk to it and *hug it*. Pets usually are willing to share affection. Of course, the affection that one shares with an animal isn't of much depth, but then the risk is also small." When we make decisions that pets are *more loving* than people, then we deny our basic need to be understood, and we retreat slightly down the road of loneliness.

2. In giving the gift of ourselves we are brought more to life. We are more in touch with our feelings. But if the motivation behind our giving is to insult others, assault their character, or in any way make them responsible for our reaction, then we have misused the gift and shown ourselves to be irresponsible and merely victims. Alternatively, if our motive has been to want understanding, then we will discover that *our own inner experience has been clarified for us.*

I have a Norwegian friend who came to America twenty-five years ago. Although he speaks fluent English today, with a delightful accent, he says that unless he occasionally converses in Norwegian with his wife, he will lose touch with his native tongue. He doesn't want to do that. We stay more alive, more in touch with our thoughts and feelings, by regularly risking an expression of them with one we feel will work to understand us. To withhold is to experience a gradual deadening. That, as previously detailed, is our basic loneliness; estrangement from our thoughts and our feeling processes. If a man is growing dead to himself, then he has no one at all.

3. Others who listen to us are not only giving back to us the gift of themselves but also are more fully brought to life. The nature of their giving is struggle, because in listening they attempt to lay aside their own biases, prejudices, and preconceived notions of us in an effort to identify with how we feel and what we think. Putting themselves in our shoes, if not in our skin, demands that they sacrifice all tendency to judge, give advice, lecture, moralize, criticize, or misunderstand. They know how important it is for us to be accepted

and appreciated for what we uniquely are. Not wishing to tarnish that uniqueness, they discover that in the process of working to understand us, new energy begins to flow within them also. They are brought more in touch with their own feelings. Further, they experience the happiness of being deeply appreciated and loved because they have accepted the gift of "me" unconditionally. In the process, then, both persons have been brought more to life, have become more in touch with their own inner resources.

5 how change affects
our loneliness

Life begins with separation—birth. It ends with separation—death. In between those two extremes we experience countless other separations.

In a single sentence: nothing living is ever the same from one minute to the next, and such change has an effect on our loneliness.

I saw this demonstrated quite dramatically some time ago. A businessman, lecturing to a group of us on the subject of change, began his talk by pulling a bright red apple from his suit pocket (in the process satisfying my curiosity about the big bulge that I had noticed there). Not knowing at first whether he was going to give it to someone in the audience to eat, or munch on it himself, he surprised us all by using a small pocket knife to slowly and methodically carve out a wedge. Saying nothing, he laid it by the side of the speaker's stand. Fully aware that the curiosity of the audience was growing during his speech, it was with a hint of amusement in his eye that, at the end, he throttled down, reached for the apple and said, "Oh, yes, the apple, do you see what has happened to it?" During his thirty-minute talk it had begun to turn brown. Time makes a change in living things.

More specifically, time brings a change in our appearance; the onset of wrinkles gives many of us no small amount of distress. Fear of growing old prompts many to devote the bulk of their energy to frantic efforts to give the continuing appearance of youth, with face-lifting as an example. In aging, our step becomes a bit slower, and on occasion we may, sometimes to our embarrassment, have to ask someone to repeat what they said; our hearing isn't what it used to be. There is a probability that our shoulders, once straight and erect, may become rounded by fatigue.

Nature? It, too, is in a constant state of change. The four seasons are accompanied by interesting variations in the landscape and weather. Of his perch high atop a mountain in the California Sierras, the late Arthur Robinson wrote, "You can't live closer to creation than this. It is like looking at the ocean—you never tire of the view, and it never looks exactly the same twice." It is possible to scan the same panorama each day, and discover something different, something that has changed.

And as we are often reminded in sudden and dramatic ways, our own little personal world is also undergoing constant change. Periodically, our roots, sunk deep down into the soil of familiarity, are torn up through separation from much-loved places and people.

But some of our most painful separations are those that time brings about within our families. It makes parents both happy and sad when others take notice of their children with, "Say, your kids are certainly growing!" The dizzy rate at which they progress from reading Charlie Brown in the comics to college catalogues is probably the phenomenon that prompts the saying, "My, but doesn't time fly?"

Frequently, and often with no warning at all, death brings sudden changes that leave the remaining family members numb with grief. Separation, constant separation. It happens that no sooner have we begun to adjust to one than we are jolted by another.

But the nature of our relationships is also constantly changing. This is because two individuals are always changing. There is no one permanent "me." There are ten thousand real "me's," because we are changing daily. There is one real me today and there will be another real me tomorrow. As a result, understanding and love between two people is either regressing or deepening. This means that the degree and intensity of our individual loneliness is forever in a state of flux. In our relations with our mates, children, parents, and friends, we are experiencing a greater or lesser degree of loneliness today compared with yesterday.

John Powell writes: "I discover that this business of telling you who I am cannot be done once and for all. I must *continually* tell you who I am and you must *continually* tell me who you are, because both of us are continually evolving."[1] He is right.

Unless intimates daily tell each other who they are in response to places, events, and people, they will gradually become strangers. The person you talked to yesterday is not the same person today.

Time also changes the quality of our experiences. It is impossible to recapture or recreate the exact same mood, excitement, or atmosphere of a particular experience now past. In no way can we relive it now as we experienced it then. Oh, we can try, but somehow the *quality* of the experience will be different. Time dictates that. Think of all the time and effort we waste in attempting to duplicate exciting and memorable past events.

When I reflect on some of the good times that our family has enjoyed down through the years, I see that these good times were not always planned in advance. Sometimes they

[1] John Powell, *Why Am I Afraid to Tell You Who I Am?* (Chicago: Peacock Books, 1969).

simply happened. A careful rehearsal of what is to come can easily stifle the type of spontaneity and creativity that makes life an adventure. When our life-style at all times becomes *predictable*, a certain spirit of adventure is lost. For instance, when we attempt to duplicate a past memorable occasion the situation becomes artificial; we are more involved with the past than we are with the present.

Several years ago my wife, four daughters, and I spent a week by the ocean in Southern California. The month was August and those who say that the waves there are at their boiling best during that month are correct. They were. A number of people were body-surfing, bobbing up and down in the water like so many corks, maneuvering to catch the top of a foam-capped breaker and then riding it in until it crashed on the shore. Sometimes they miscalculated and were thrown to the ocean floor, propelled fiercely along the bottom . . . finally surfacing with ugly red sandburns etched into their skin. I tried it . . . got the same treatment . . . but still found it to be the most fun I had had in a long time. As a matter of fact it was so much fun that we decided to go back to the same spot on the beach a year later. But from the outset it was different. At first we had high hopes. The place was the same, the waves were almost as high, but the *quality* of the experience was different. We were let down, if not depressed. Walking dejectedly back to the car we jointly decided that it was futile to try to relive a previous delight.

Time changes things; time changes people; time changes the nature of our individual moods and expectations. Precious and memorable moments are not meant to be relived or recaptured. This is for a purpose. It allows that moment to remain forever unique and unmatched.

In the same vein, it is impossible to take up with people in the same spirit and fashion with which we left them, whether five years or five days ago. We remember them as being one way. But in the interim we have all changed.

Recently, on a short holiday, we rejoined old friends for the purpose of renewing the relationship. What happened the first day was something that we had not planned—deep sharing and intimacy. Intimacy, if genuine, is never anticipated in advance. It simply flows spontaneously in keeping with our needs at the moment. Just before supper we decided to go our separate ways, but before doing so we agreed to get together on the following day. "It will be fun to take up where we left off today," someone said. When the time came I was still basking in the good feelings of our previous meeting. But what came out of the next get-together was what I considered to be a monotonous rehearsal of the events of that first day. In reality it was probably not monotonous at all, but because I was so intent on trying to recapture the magic of our first meeting I wasn't in tune with the mood of the moment. Every experience of intimacy has a unique quality of its own. Time dictates a change that makes that so.

Dietrich Bonhoeffer, a clergyman who spent several years in a concentration camp in Germany during World War II, wrote in his book *Letters and Papers from Prison*[2] that there is nothing that can fill the gap when we are away from those we love and that it would be wrong to try. Speaking out of his own personal experience, he said that even God cannot fill that gap. Irreligious? Some may say so. But no person can ever be *replaced*; it is impossible to find another exact duplicate. If that were possible something would be taken away from the uniqueness of the original relationship.

You may be asking what this type of change has to do with aloneness and loneliness. Through the years we are separated from good friends, loved ones, and familiar places. Many times this separation brings about an unexpected, sudden, and bewildering experience of *aloneness*. With each separation there is a type of aloneness experience that is unique to a particular

[2] Dietrich Bonhoeffer, *Letters and Papers from Prison* (New York: Macmillan, 1967).

person or place. This is as it should be. The sanctity of a memorable moment or relationship is preserved only to the extent that we do not attempt to recapture it with another person in the present.

Separation from those we love deeply brings change, but that change does not mean the pain of separation should be eased by trying to forget. Dwelling on the past is not a good thing, but when memories come flooding in, it is sensible to allow ourselves the luxury of accepting them.

But in such separations from natural events there can also be a great loneliness, or a fear of loving again. Sometimes when we have loved deeply there is a resolve never to go through a similar pain of separation. "All love eventually ends in suffering."[3] When we love, the death of one terminates the relationship. That means suffering and an experience of aloneness. But it can evolve into loneliness if we decide that we will never love again.

For many of us it takes a good deal of giving, testing, probing, risking, and exploration in the process of fusion that is involved in a growing relationship of trust. It is only after such a period that we finally trust enough to be willing to say, "Here I am, I open myself up to you because now I trust you with what I am." That process of probing and exploration is sometimes long; at other times it is short. We go through it many times in life. If there are repeated separations from trusted and loved intimates, we may decide that all the effort expended in achieving closeness is not worth it. The pain of separation (or the prospect of it) is too great. We choose *not* to love again. That will be a responsible choice if we do not bemoan the consequences—that is, play "poor me." If, however, we become lonely and blame others for our lot in life, then it will be an irresponsible choice. If the latter, then we can do something about it. We can choose to risk loving again.

[3] Clark E. Moustakas, *Loneliness* (Englewood Cliffs, N.J.: Prentice-Hall, Inc., 1961), p. 101.

6 making the most of
our aloneness

"I'm alone sometimes but rarely do I feel lonely." To be able to make the distinction between those two realities is the base from which we *begin* to assume the responsibility for our lives.

Of all the human situations in which we find ourselves, being alone is commonly seen as having the least value. "Me" —especially if we don't like "me"—can be the most boring, if not the most frightening person of all to confront. Not surprisingly, it isn't unusual to dread being alone. Why? Because then all we have is ourselves. That might mean being faced with unpleasant feelings of guilt, anger, fear, discontent, gross inadequacy, and helplessness. If we are running from those parts of our person the prospect of times of aloneness will be unwelcome, possibly frightening.

True, we need a trusted companion or friend, someone with whom we can share love, but intimacy must be counter-balanced with aloneness. The choices and decisions that we make in our times of aloneness are ours and ours alone. We tap our own inner resources and make decisions that only we can make, in the process coming more gradually to trust our own resources.

Our first aloneness experience

The birth experience is our first aloneness experience. Note: not loneliness, but aloneness. Separated *physically*, we are not later able to recall that moment of birth, but we frequently relive thereafter the feelings of anxiety and helplessness that accompanied the first experience of aloneness. The repeated physical separations that occur in life's natural events may continue to provoke that initial anxiety. Through self understanding and awareness we can turn down the volume on those feelings but there is no way of guaranteeing that we can do away with them once and for all. If we understand this, it helps us not to panic if we should find ourselves in a state of anxiety following a separation.

Separation anxiety

The familiar "separation anxiety" experienced by people— children and adults alike—is an attack that occurs after physical separations from familiar and loved places, people, things, pets, anything at all to which we have been closely attached. Granger Westberg in his little book *Good Grief*[1] describes the stages of anxiety and grief that accompany any type of loss. The nature of our separations varies. Some are by choice, but others are not.

For example, because we wish to live in closer proximity to relatives or close friends for reasons of health, or because of a desire to live in a climate more to our liking, we may as a family agree to move. At other times we may have to move because our employment demands it. A promotion, larger salary, a bigger house on the horizon, are tasty prospects, yet the move itself is not of our choice.

Further, separation from a job, retirement, loss of a home

[1] Granger E. Westberg, *Good Grief* (Philadelphia: Fortress Press, 1962).

through fire or flood, loss of sight or hearing, or separation through death can all arouse that initial feeling of anxiety and aloneness that accompanies the birth experience. As the infant casts about for ways of dealing with his separation anxiety, it isn't difficult to understand that he will attach himself to things and places, commonly referred to as roots. The familiar "security blanket" is one such compensation. A type of security is also found in a doll, one's thumb, or a toy. In this also lies the value of a pet. In its company, therefore, we turn down the volume on our fear of abandonment and separation.

In our aloneness we associate security with places. A child soon becomes familiar with his or her room, its smells and sounds (wind in the screen, branches brushing against the house, traffic sounds outside). Many a youngster, uprooted from such familiar experiences, because of a move, is stricken with anxiety and despair for months afterward.

Birdman of Alcatraz[2] describes how a man, sentenced to a lifetime of solitary confinement, chose to pass his time of aloneness. His birds not only provided him with a type of companionship, but in experimenting with them he contributed a storehouse of new and interesting scientific data on bird life itself. Such creativity, advances, and discoveries often flow out of the acceptance and use of our aloneness.

Immediately following separation from a husband or wife through death, it is not uncommon for the remaining partner to travel back to the place where the mate was born, where they first met and courted, were married, or spent their early married years together. It is another attempt to go back to a place where at one time there were feelings of great security. Going back home to familiar and once-loved places is a way of dealing with aloneness anxiety.

It is self-deceptive to imagine that any *lasting* security can be found in a place, object, or pet, but its temporary value

[2] T. E. Gaddis, *Birdman of Alcatraz* (New York: Random House, 1955).

must be recognized. As we slowly discover, however, that our security lies within and not "out there" in a place or thing, we will also discover that our fear of abandonment and the severity of our anxiety attacks are lessening.

It was refreshing recently for me to revisit the little prairie town in which I spent my Huckleberry Finn years. One of my first visits was to the grain mill and a visit with the eighty-year-old man whom I had admired as a boy. He cupped his hands behind his head, reflected for a minute as he sat with feet propped up on his desk, and said, "You know something . . . I've never owned a car in my life." As if that wasn't hard enough to believe, he went on to say that in this small town it was possible to walk to the grocery store, church, athletic events, and his place of work. "I have always been content in doing only that," he said. He ventured out of town on the train or in a car a few times with one of his children, but for the most part he was content simply to enjoy the familiar places and people that he had come to know and love during his long life. Some might say that he lacked a certain inquisitiveness and spirit that make life an adventure. But who are we to judge? It is the privilege of every man to choose what it is that gives him the greatest contentment and peace.

It is said that one of the reasons for the increase in mental illness today is the increasing mobility of the American people. One in five families picks up and moves every year, if not across country then across town or state. This means that we are continually being uprooted from that which is familiar to us. Such separations produce a great deal of anxiety and depression.

Loners

Sometimes we have difficulty in understanding loners, those people who choose this mode of living as a life-style. I am thinking of the times that I have asked such individuals, "How can you stand being so much alone?" I have asked it of farmers whose homes have been located far off the beaten path. I asked it once of a lighthouse keeper on the north shore of Lake Superior in Minnesota. Another time I asked it of a little old weather-beaten goatherder. Day after day in every type of conceivable weather, pelting rain or blistering sun, bone-chilling northwesters, or blast-furnace heat, he could be seen alone, tending his goats in the fields. Sometimes he and his little band of followers meandered past my office window. When they stopped to feed he would stop with them and wait patiently. He had given each of them a name and he could be heard speaking to them as if they were his own children. They in turn responded to him in a manner befitting children who knew that they were loved. One rainy day, as he stood erect under a tree, with his familiar staff in his hand, I called out to him, "How can you stand being alone all the time?" His answer was a smile . . . as he pointed his staff to the "children" that surrounded him. He seemed to be saying that companionship with any living thing can ease our aloneness pain. Maybe this is one reason the farmer feels a type of fulfillment. In plowing the soil and watching crops grow, he is bringing new things to life.

Can you remember some of your first childhood experiences of aloneness? If so, are you able to remember what, if anything, you learned or discovered during those moments? Particularly vivid to me is the childhood memory of coming downstairs one morning to find my pet goldfish floating dead on top of the water. I was five. That little pet had become my fast friend. I had fed him faithfully for two years and it had been great fun to poke my finger at the side of the bowl and watch his mouth open as he reached out for my finger. On the days that he zigzagged wildly back and forth in the bowl he seemed to know I was watching him perform. When he died I was crushed. The sudden separation was devastating. At first my parents tried to console me, but it didn't help. In my aloneness grief behind the garage I carefully laid the fragile fish in a cigar box and placed it in a hole that I had chopped out of the frozen Minnesota earth. But out of that separation experience there eventually came a new inquisitiveness about death; questions that I probably would not have asked had I not experienced this first separation.

If we allow it, it is in our moments of aloneness that new thoughts, discoveries, and appreciations can arise. I also have a memory of the day, during World War II, that my best friend, Clinton, together with his family, boarded a train and headed for their new home on the West Coast. On that dreaded day we stood on the platform together and through tears talked of when we would see each other again. As I watched the train pull away and begin to snake its way across the prairie, memories of all our adventures together came flooding over me. When I could no longer see the train on the horizon, only a trail of smoke, it seemed as if my own little personal world had been shattered again. Another separation with which I had to contend . . . feelings of abandonment . . . aloneness . . . isolation. But in the prolonged period of aloneness and grief that followed, there eventually emerged a new appreciation of friendship, not just with that one friend, but friendship with all people.

In and through all of our many and varied experiences of separation, whether by choice or not, can come a gradual and frequently painful awareness that security is not to be found in a place, thing, or object outside ourselves. "Going back" may revive pleasant feelings and memories, but there is nothing lasting in that. During those times that we are better able to accept and fully experience our aloneness, no matter from whom or what we have been separated, and whether by choice or not, the resulting discoveries can add new dimensions to our lives.

In the final analysis, others can assist us only up to a certain point. They can help us along the way; give us encouragement, help us sift through various options in the face of an important decision, but then we will have to accept the reality of our aloneness and realize that no one but we ourselves can make the decision that has to be made.

Those in positions of great responsibility are frequently made aware of this reality. Despite the fact that they may be surrounded by a bevy of brains trusts (brilliant men from whom they can seek advice and counsel), in the end, only one person can make the decision.

The aloneness of single mothers

One by-product of the rising divorce rate in our country in the 1970's is the plight of single mothers trying to cope with the frustrations of rearing children *alone*. While social and economic discrimination is leveled against them, what is even worse and more painful is that there is no other adult in the house with whom to share the concerns and decisions. A recent article in the Sacramento *Bee* described a new pioneer effort to bring single mothers together in the hope of coming up with some sort of a solution. At a meeting in Berkeley, some of their problems were spelled out; one important one being that total commitment to children is frustrating to many single mothers who often think they are inadequate and incapable of rearing their children alone. Should they treat former husbands as ex-husband, friend, father of the children, and which of these relationships would be of greatest benefit to the children?

Judy, a divorcée with two sons, said, "If I were living with my husband I wonder if my children would be calmer. I worry about it all the time." Establishing a relationship with a new man can prove difficult. "There's a whole different relationship with a man," one woman said. "It's usually sexual, not platonic. Men think you're an easy mark. You have to tell the men you meet that you have children. For this reason the easiest men to relate to are married men who have children. No matter how much you like the guy, it's really important that he like your kids. You ask yourself not if he can fit into *my* life but into *our* life."

If there is a husband-less mother on a street, her children are the most apt to be blamed for any disturbance, merely because there is no father. "Every time a garbage can is kicked over," one mother said angrily, "my children are blamed."

And then there are financial woes. Single mothers earn less than men.

Another divorced woman said: "When you live on your own, after the kids have gone to bed at night you crave adult companionship, anyone at all to talk to."

The solution: Two or more single mothers are experimenting . . . moving in together . . . working out a contract in which they can share responsibility for their children, and enjoy each other's companionship. "There's no competition. We're two adult people. There's no male-female squabble and no role-playing as there is in most marriages when kids are around."

Summary

Almost everything in life is geared toward togetherness, no matter how superficial or artificial. We do not allow ourselves much time in which to experience our aloneness. To have ourselves is to have our thoughts and feelings. If we like them and accept them, we will make the most of our aloneness. If we do not like them, aloneness will be frightening. What a man thinks and feels is uniquely his. He is entitled to experience both fully.

That might mean being alone in a meadow, bending over to smell a wild rose and simply allowing that which is within him to respond. The memories and feelings that accompanied the original discovery of such simple beauty in boyhood begin to flow. The result? Renewed appreciation of life's simple and basic things.

But if our aloneness experiences are not by choice, but come from the flow of natural events, over which we have no control, there are two options: (a) In not allowing ourselves to accept them the separation can defeat us and leave us in a state of unresolved despair for the rest of our lives, deciding that we will never risk loving again; (b) Allowing ourselves to accept our aloneness experiences serves ultimately to bring out our best possibilities. It can give us time to evaluate our goals, the quality of our work, values, and faith and can lead us to new appreciation of our husbands and wives, friends, or God.

7 assuming personal responsibility for loving

"When are you *ever* going to grow up?" is the charge leveled by parents at their teen-agers who regularly leave six layers of clothing draped over their bedroom chairs. This may be countered by the teen-agers, saying, "Dad, you sure act like a baby most of the time . . . always expecting Mom to wait on you." Maturity—another of those words that seem to defy a single definition—is likely to be viewed by a girl as the day she is first allowed to wear make-up. A boy could well see it as the time his parents first allow him to back the family car out of the driveway. To the "grownup," maturity is most often measured by the number of birthdays we have had. Yet, many a forty-year-old man is just as irresponsible and dependent as is his fifteen-year-old son.

Mainly, then, we associate maturity with chronological age. Along with that we acquire added responsibility and privileges. The term rites of passage has been coined to describe those events and milestones in life when we give our children added responsibility and privileges, confirmation often being one such rite of passage. Such an occasion usually merits our first suit, generally ill-fitted, or very expensive dress and possibly high heels. One young lad saw confirmation as his first gigantic step toward manhood. After the affair was over, he manfully strode to the rear of the church and, in the presence of several awestruck classmates, proceeded to light up his first cigarette, in the process burning his fingers on the match.

Proceeding up the ladder, another rite of passage takes place at sixteen. We are permitted to apply for a driver's license and with greater frequency hint around for use of the family car. At eighteen, young people, with mixed emotions and packed bags, leave home, some to serve in the military, others to go to college or work . . . but all now to vote.

Because of our misconception that maturity is simply a matter of adding years to life, we do not always understand that pain and frustration accompany growth. If maturity were but a matter of totting up the number of birthday candles that we blow out on our cake each year—with the additional new privileges—it would be a relatively painless matter. But it isn't. Perhaps a bit of that pain is reflected in the frustration of the seven-year-old boy who, after being told to sit in the corner for having slapped his younger sister, mumbled, "Mom, I may be sitting down on the outside but I'm still standing up on the inside."

One of the ways in which we grow is by coming up against obstacles that demand evaluation, struggle, and risk. If we try to escape the consequences of these risks we remain helpless and dependent children.

If you will fantasize with me for a moment, think of a tiny, uninhabited island far out in the Pacific Ocean. The men who first come to her shores are dependent upon outside help to keep them alive. Food and supplies are shipped in with regularity. But slowly the new inhabitants begin to develop their own resources, planting and harvesting, done with much back-breaking labor. In the process they are becoming less dependent upon outside help to sustain them. That is the painful type of transition which accompanies growth, edging away from dependence on outside resources to dependence and trust on our own.

Human growth, then, is the gradual movement away from the posture of the dependent child whose need is *to be loved* to the adult who wants *to give love.* That movement goes on for a lifetime. Along the way it involves being hurt, hurting, feeling misunderstood, judged, criticized, knowing failure, heartache, and rejection. But in the process of learning and risking to *give* love we slowly begin to rise above some of the agonizing fears of love.

Maneuvering desperately, some try to escape the pain of growth, looking for shortcuts and ways around the struggle. They feel that by virtue of their good looks, personality, position, status, connections, money, experience, or age, things should come to them without struggle, discipline, frustration, or pain. It is easy to forget that few important reforms have ever been worked out in a day; few great men discover their full power in a single brilliant achievement; few inventions work well on the first trial. Slow experimentation, frequent failure, delay, opposition, and obstacles lie along the road to success, achievement, and human growth. These incidents are constant reminders that we acquire character out of growth even more than material reward.

Erich Fromm in *The Art of Loving*[1] says that the child up to the age of ten only *responds* gratefully to *being loved.* At that point he begins for the first time to create love by something that he does. We may disagree on exactly when this transition takes place in the life of the child, but there does come a time early in life when he begins to create love by something that he does. I remember when our children first began to bring home their primitive drawings and poems from kindergarten. It was with a great deal of delight and anticipation that they gave them to us, at the same time watching

---

[1] Erich Fromm, *The Art of Loving* (New York: Harper, 1956).

for our reactions. Their faces would light up whenever we Scotch-taped one to the refrigerator or on the bulletin board. At moments such as this the child becomes aware of the fact that when you create love by something that you do and give, then as a by-product you are getting something back for yourself—a pat on the head, a word of praise, a thank you, smile, or look of pleasure; not always of course but most of the time. If the creations of our children are ignored or not fully appreciated, their hurt is apt to prompt them to retreat again. That type of decision, each time it is made, contributes to a renewal of their fear of loving, with its accompanying loneliness.

Super good guys

Each of us has a genuine "good guy" inside. It is the part of us that loves someone for no other reason than we simply want to love them. There is no thought of getting anything in return, no "What's in it for me?" and we are not trying to make ourselves lovable.

But super good guys are different. Their motivation in dealing with others is to *make* themselves lovable. THE EMOTION BEHIND IT IS FEAR, probably a grim sense of duty, and nearcrippling feelings of responsibility. The motto is: Be loved at all costs to yourself.

Super good guys seldom have the courage to speak out, fearing they might make themselves unlovable. Throughout history they have never invented anything, led a revolution, or challenged the status quo. Constantly needing security from smiles, handshakes, and pats on the back, they feel desperately that they must be loved by all. They will boast, "Some of my best friends are Negroes," but then proceed to put their homes up for sale if a black person moves in next door. The possibility of their being fired from a job is remote. They don't have the courage to stand up and be counted for any ideals. To do so might mean rocking the boat, and they can't risk that. They survive only through the props of ego building from patient spouses or members of their families who know when and how to apply the soft soap. They will be paraded through a corridor of lilies to their death with a smile on their faces (a plastered-on permanent smile that they have worn all their lives), their only mission in life accomplished—that everyone sang their praises.

Super good guys gain their goals of collective love at the expense of the world, which has paid dearly for their needs, while real men have struggled and died.

Somehow they are always dull and predictable; responses are automatic and in keeping with what is expected of them. Thinking of themselves as expert listeners, they hear only the *words* of others and are unable to identify with the feelings behind the words. This is because they are preoccupied with their own feelings of fear.

A typical "super good guy transaction" is apt to go something like this:

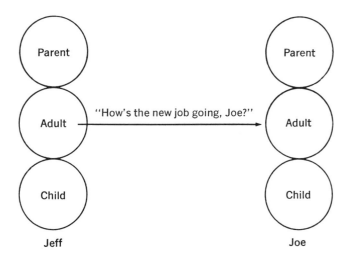

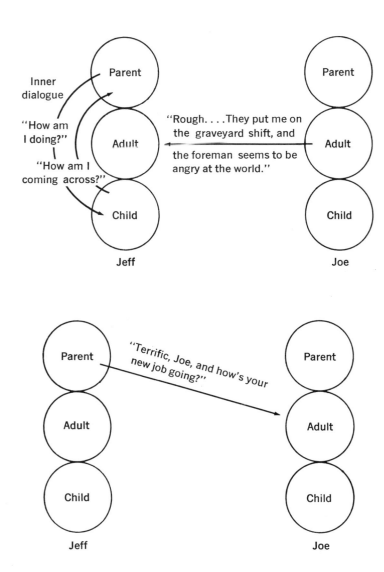

In listening, Jeff is so preoccupied with his own inner dialogue that his Adult is not tuned in or aware of the response. *His* response, out of his Parent, is programmed, ritualistic, and nonthinking in nature. What he thinks of as a burning compassion for Joe is nothing more than another frantic effort to satisfy his own insatiable need to be lovable. His entire lifestyle, mode of dress, manners, and speech are designed with one purpose in mind: I'VE GOT TO MAKE MYSELF LOVABLE.

The super good guy, then, is both frightened and lonely. He has never moved away from the status of the frightened little boy that he once was.

The slow transition from *needing to be loved* to *wanting to love* involves pain, frustration, and risk. Much is contingent upon the willingness, ability, and readiness of others to receive it. At times when there is little or no response, we may feel misunderstood or rejected, even though this may not be the case at all. Again, our old tapes are replaying.

Loving and its responsibilities

Love isn't really love until it is given away, but it isn't merely a matter of loving. It also involves learning the *responsibility* that accompanies loving. The nature of that responsibility is such that when we love we always make allowance for the response happening in the way it is going to happen. We can never predict the response in advance. When we love it is frequently accompanied by a fantasy of the way in which we would like to have our gift received, or the manner in which we would like to be loved in return. But in loving we are not consciously on the lookout for a particular type of response, nor do we rehearse in advance the manner in which love should come back to us. In this fashion, if the response is a bland one, or even none at all, we will not be crushed or "read in" rejection. It was simply a risk that we took for no other reason than we wanted to love. Love does not need reasons to love. If there happens to be a positive response to our loving in the form of a smile that is returned, a word of appreciation, a hug of gratitude, or the appearance of any new life at all, then it is a pleasant surprise. In a sense, ANY RESPONSE TO OUR LOVING MUST ALWAYS BE A PLEASANT SURPRISE. The extent that it is so determines the degree to which we may have rehearsed our expectations.

This is the case even with loved ones. There is never any guarantee that love will be returned. But when it is we discover what lies at the heart of loving; in giving something of ourselves that is returned, as a *by-product,* our need to be loved is also mysteriously met. That is the paradox of loving.

So, in loving, we are *sometimes* loved in return, but not always. Our giving occasionally meets with hostility, resentment, indifference, suspicion, ingratitude, and misunderstanding. But when it is accepted and valued, the response automatically fulfills our need to be loved. This is the nature of the I'M OK position.

It is deceptive to think that we are lonely only when we haven't gotten enough attention. That is the feeling of the little child. He experiences loneliness when he feels that he has not gotten the love he needs. But to feel, as grownups, that we have not gotten enough love probably means that we have been sitting and waiting, hoping that others will take the initiative, will come to us and give us compliments, praise, encouragement, bolstering, and support. In fact, we are not giving of ourselves because we are afraid to take the risk, or we are lazy, or know nothing about giving love. Still thinking of ourselves as the center of the universe, around whom everyone should want to flock, our interest revolves around ways of meeting our own needs and not the needs of others.

The loneliest people are those who have decided to stop loving. Yes, it is a choice. It is of our own doing. We may sometimes say that we have good reasons for doing so. But whenever we do, it is because we have allowed ourselves to be hurt to the point where we actually believe "it's all their fault." VICTIMS ALWAYS FEEL LONELY. As long as we keep justifying or defending our position, there is no hope of taking that first step.

Legend has it that an army general, together with his troops, stormed a walled fortress in England. Using ladders, they scaled the walls and dropped down on the other side. The general, who was the last one over, then kicked away all the ladders, thus ensuring no possible avenue of retreat. The men would conquer the fortress or die in the attempt.

Human growth is the process of gradually kicking away all the ladders by which we might retreat from personal responsibility for our decisions, feelings, and behavior. As long as we play the role of victim, blaming others, events, or circumstances for our loneliness, we will continue to need the ladder of irresponsibility. Regardless of the manner in which we have reacted to events and people in the past, we are responsible now, today. For that reason, today is the first day of the rest of our lives.

8 loneliness and time

Within each of us there is a structure hunger that must be satisfied. If it isn't, it will produce boredom, depression, and loneliness. That hunger is most clearly evidenced in the question that we ask ourselves and others, "What do I do with myself until the next TV show at 9:00 P.M., until bedtime, until school resumes on Monday, my husband comes home from work, vacation ends, winter is over," etc.

The teen-ager, coming in the door after school, may ask his mother, "What is there to do until supper?" It could well be that she may have planned something for her son or daughter to do; an errand downtown or some chore around the house. Depending upon the teen-ager's mood or need at the moment, his mother's suggestion may lead to resentment or to relief; resentment if there has been no free time at all during the day, but relief if the teen-ager has no idea whatsoever how the next several hours can be spent.

Most of our time is structured for us by other institutions— school, work, and church. It is when we have free time on our hands that we ask, "Now what do I do with myself until . . . ?"

Children find that the bulk of their time is structured for them. In school the schedule calls for a set number of class hours a day. Recess is the only time in which finding ways to pass time may pose a problem. If there is a fear of love, a youngster may withdraw. Others will plunge into a vigorous game of softball, while still others will choose to talk quietly to classmates near the drinking fountain. It all depends upon their individual moods, needs, and feelings at the moment.

The housewife's time is well structured for her, too. In her dual role as wife and mother there are always a variety of jobs that require her attention and take up her time. She cannot be fired if she is slovenly. What may sometimes surprise her, even amaze her, is that when longed-for unstructured moments are at hand, she may be lost. "I have this free time . . . now how in the world do I spend it?" She may even discover that the time is best spent in sleeping.

The bulk of the husband's time is structured for him also. However, being in business provides a type of diversity that his wife does not know at home. Therefore, he may not experience the boredom of sameness that she does.

The alcoholic *is* alcoholic in part because he does not know how to structure his time. As long as others are structuring it for him at home or on the job he may stay sober. The same holds true of his recreation. When people are entertaining him, he isn't bored. But at the end of the ninth inning, when the last vendor has hawked his wares and the last player has left the field, he is once again at a loss. "Now what do I do with myself?" At that point he heads for a bar.

But we also speak of being bored with people: "Jane just bores me to death." If we spend most of our working hours with people, we will probably need to spend our unstructured time alone—painting, reading, or working quietly in the carpentry shop. Too, if the competition and oneupmanship in the office drain all of our energies, we may want and need to experience intimacy with people during the time we are away from the office.

Therefore, we will not be doing the same things during our unstructured moments. The nature of our work, our individual temperaments, family situation, age, and health determine what best meets our emotional and physical needs during those hours.

To do the same things over and over again in our unstructured moments can bring on boredom also. Some people always head for the tennis courts, others always go to the movies; yet others always beat a path to the pool table in the family room. They may enjoy what they are doing but in exercising more than one option during their unstructured hours, people tap their many inner resources—creativity, spirit of adventure, curiosity, and spontaneity.

We have various options when it comes to ways in which we may choose to structure our time. Most of them provide us with ways of being *with* people. For some that is enough; particularly if we are afraid of love. Others will want to get beyond the polite formalities into the area of intimacy.

PASTIMES

Pastimes provide us with a way of being with people, both in getting and in giving strokes. Parent in nature, "small talk," "shooting the breeze," and "passing the time of day," usually revolve around "safe" subjects, often judgmental in nature. Though strokes are tossed back and forth, they are likely to be of the marshmallow variety, but they are better than none at all. Some people are excellent pastimers . . . and have the reputation for being such. "What a talker." Others hate to make small talk. Poor pastimers, their fears mount as knowledge of current events, gossip, sports, babies, etc., begins to dwindle. Conversation, progressing down to a painful dribble, may abruptly stop . . . and it is that moment of silence that the poor pastimers dread. *They fear moments of silence, times when no one is saying anything.* One reason for this is that they feel responsible not only for keeping the conversation going but also interesting. This is so that they will be interesting to others. During those mortifying moments of silence, with eyes riveted on the floor or occasionally meeting the glance of his fellow pastimer, he discovers that instead of enjoying the silence, a very heavy dialogue is set in motion between his inner Parent and Child.

"I'll bet he *really* thinks I'm stupid now. Here I stand with nothing more to say."

"If I hadn't started talking to him in the first place I wouldn't have gotten into this mess. How do I get out of here?"

The silence and resulting "kick me" inner dialogue that blares away inside himself only confirms once more what he felt and feared all along—I'M REALLY UNLOVABLE.

Pastimes are always of a superficial nature. Yet they are important because they can be ways of warming up to something more personal and intimate. On the other hand, this may never happen. Two people, yes, sometimes even in marriage, may never get beyond small talk. Forever skirting around "risk," husband and wife may pass the time of day for an hour after supper, but then one settles down behind the newspaper and the other takes to the telephone. Such people are lonely. There is no risk involved in pastimes. The persons involved confine the conversation to polite exchanges not generally subject to value judgments, criticism, or hurts.

RITUALS

Rituals are different from pastimes. A ritual is a fixed or set way of passing time. Some of the most familiar are greeting rituals. They may be of the simplest variety:

"Good morning, Anne."

"You're looking good, John."

This is considered to be a two-stroke ritual. Even though Anne and John were only passing each other on the street, that two-second exchange provided a way by which they could pass that brief moment and exchange strokes. Again, the strokes were not of the 100 percent pure gold variety, but nevertheless they were strokes.

Each person has his or her stock greeting rituals, most frequently the ones that were observed, heard, and picked up from parents.

Others may choose to exchange recognition through the medium of a kiss or hug. It has become a ritual. The same may be said of shaking hands. Not infrequently it provides the only physical contact that we have with people. It is safe in nature. If we are frightened at the prospect of touching or hugging a good friend or relative, shaking hands at least provides us with a way of experiencing some of the good feelings that go hand in hand with physical contact. A holdover from childhood, physical strokes always seem to best satisfy our attention needs.

One can imagine the dismay that would be felt if, on a given Sunday morning, the minister of a church announced: "As of today I am going to dispense with handshaking at the church door at the conclusion of the service." Shaking hands with the minister, a long-standing ritual, often provides the one and only safe way in which church members may touch their minister. To the layman, the "stroke value" inherent in this handshake, based upon a value scale of zero to 100 percent, probably ranks near 95 percent.

Consider all the different types of rituals: Saturday night rituals, Sunday morning rituals, weekend rituals, worship rituals, bathroom rituals, eating rituals, vacation rituals. If we do not have enough daily rituals, we may need to work on some. Some couples make it a point of eating out every Friday night. A housewife may look forward to 1:00 P.M. every afternoon because then she can ease into her favorite chair, drink a cup of coffee, and watch her favorite television program. It is a ritual.

It is particularly important to have rituals when we are on vacation. Even though we talk about and plan our vacations long in advance, still we are frequently surprised to discover that once well into a vacation we are bored. The problem could be that we do not have enough rituals.

I remember as a boy the rituals that centered on our one-month vacation at the summer cabin. They had not varied for decades. One generation seemed to inherit the rituals of the preceding generation. There was the ice truck that lumbered into camp every afternoon at 1:30 P.M. We would wait by the bridge and jump on it as it went by. Sometimes, the iceman let us help chip off chunks for iceboxes. At 3:00 P.M. the young campers would converge on the beach. Our mothers in turn would dress up in their summer finery and get together for a *kaffeeklatsch,* rotating from cottage to cottage each day. At 7:00 P.M. a goodly number of campers emerged from their havens in the woods for an evening stroll, exchanging verbal pleasantries as they passed one another along the tree-shaded rural road. The final ritual of the day found members of our family sitting on a darkened front porch watching the sunset through a large picture window that had been installed especially for that purpose. Many times that meant sitting in the dark long after the sun had gone down, listening quietly to the loons on the lake, talking about the events of the day, or reliving some memory out of the past. "Remember when?" That type of pastime is particularly necessary on vacation. Without pastimes we would become bored. Rituals, no matter how tedious, are better than just sitting.

WITHDRAWAL

Withdrawal is another choice that we have with time. Sometimes we withdraw from people in order to experience our aloneness, at other times because we are afraid of love.

Warren Harding, the adventurous mountain climber who scaled the sheer face of El Capitan in Yosemite Valley, alludes to the benefits that accompany the times we choose to withdraw. Speaking of his experience, he said:

It's so different up there. You're so removed, so isolated. It seems like the things you don't care about disappear; at least that happened to me. Things I care about I think about very much; the people I love, people I like, things I like to do; things I can't do right at that particular time. I missed my girl very much. I missed many of my good friends so much. I even missed my car. There are things you notice, like hawks. I even noticed an eagle one day soaring around. We heard little frogs croaking. They live up in the rocks. Little things like that.

Those twenty-seven days he spent on El Capitan were withdrawal by choice. Even though he was with another climber, he seemed to experience his aloneness fully.

James Cross, the kidnapped British diplomat who spent two months in the hands of Canadian terrorists, said of his experience in isolation: "One thing this dreadful period has given me is a sense of the importance of the ordinary things we take for granted—to live with one's family, to talk with one's friends and to breathe fresh air." Sometimes isolation is forced upon us. Yet, even out of that, new awareness and appreciations can emerge.

But we also withdraw because we are afraid of love. When we do we may think, "I really don't want things to be this way," but our fears are so overwhelming that we are literally in a state of helplessness, sometimes terror.

WORK

Work is another way of passing time. Since work is frequently performed with others it also provides us with a way of giving and getting strokes.

But it is possible to become a work addict, too. Work addicts don't always *want* to work; in fact they sometimes hate it. They *have* to work. It isn't that others demand that they do; they demand it of themselves. Known as conscientious, diligent, hard-working people on the job, they are sometimes the most bored people during their unstructured moments, fidgeting, nibbling, nitpicking . . . and complaining. Since they feel guilty unless they are always productive, they work themselves to a frazzle in an effort to get the strokes that their Not OK Child needs. *Work addicts are almost always stroke addicts.* But with work addicts, incoming strokes do not register. The stroke-recycling machine in their Not OK Child sees to that. As they are so often afraid of love, work provides them with a way of being with people, being stroked. But even though they are stroked well and often, there never are enough strokes to fill either their main stroke bucket or their auxiliary one.

GAMES

The concept of games was first outlined by Eric Berne, pioneer of Transactional Analysis. Simply stated, a game is a series of transactions between two people leading to a definite payoff—feelings of rejection, disappointment, anger, guilt, or hurt. The type of game that we play is dependent upon our life position. The life position in turn determines the type of payoff that is needed.

Berne says that the question is not, are games right or wrong? Rather, are they the best option in this situation at the moment? Sometimes they are. At Folsom State Prison, where I worked for a time as volunteer counselor, games are often the best option, if one wants to stay alive. "If I don't go along with a lot of the games in this place it is more than likely I'll end up with a knife in my back someday in the shower," one inmate confided fearfully.

In the I'M NOT OK—YOU'RE OK position, the games "Poor me" and "Ain't it awful" have as a payoff the collection of more feelings of guilt, rejection, and hurt; further reinforcing the feeling of being unlovable or not deserving love.

I'M OK—YOU'RE NOT OK. In this position the games "If it

weren't for you," "See what you made me do," and "It's all your fault" lead to an ultimate payoff of anger so that the player will be able to reinforce his own mistrust of people.

I'M NOT OK—YOU'RE NOT OK. Any game played here leads to a payoff of more despair and continued withdrawal.

I'M OK—YOU'RE OK. The game-free position, where there is a collection of gold stamps (good feelings).

It is entirely true that if we are frightened of love and intimacy, games provide us with ways of spending time with people, yet stopping short of intimacy. The majority of our time is taken up with pastimes, work, withdrawal, rituals, and games. They *may* be preludes to intimacy but they do not have to be. We can choose. The thing to remember is that fear frequently undergirds the transactions in these five ways of using time. Though they are often necessary we can become stuck there, never daring to risk intimacy.

Intimacy may be intense to the point of exhaustion. Yet it is an exhilarating exhaustion. Any attempt to prolong such moments beyond their natural course, however, can easily have the effect of negating the whole experience. There is wisdom in knowing when our time of intimacy has expended itself. We must be willing to let go, believing that there will be another time in the future.

9 loneliness within marriage and the family

Logically speaking, the least likely place for loneliness would seem to be in a setting where people live together under the same roof—in marriage and the family. This is in line with the myth that loneliness means being without people. But in our society, this disease is most rampant inside the family. In addition, the frozen aspect of loneliness is the keenest felt there. Continual physical togetherness has a way of solidifying unresolved hurts and fear. These feelings may actually abate for the short times that family members are separated through work or play. This is why weekends are often a time of crisis in homes where there is a fear of love. Let's face it, forty-eight hours with someone that we cannot or will not communicate with because of the anticipated reaction—misunderstanding or rejection—is loneliness in its most frozen state.

Isn't it true that we expect more from family members in the way of understanding? When this doesn't happen our loneliness can be severe. The intensity of our reactions to people is in direct proportion to the degree of our expectations. If we expected an acquaintance to understand us, and then found he didn't, we may be disappointed. But when a member of our own immediate family has misunderstood us, our loneliness can plunge down to its most painful level.

Sometimes our expectations at home are so high that we make no allowance for "humanness" in fellow family members. People that love us are human too.

There are days when health, weather, job difficulties, or housework contribute to fatigue, making it difficult if not sometimes impossible to understand other members of our families, let alone ourselves. When we feel this is so, it is well to give a verbal signal of some sort. "Honey, please, I'm so uptight because of a couple of things that happened at the office today that I simply am in no mood to listen now. Later, huh?" In doing so we have been honest, and others in turn will not expect more of us than we are able to give at the moment.

To be physically united but afraid of love is a dilemma that most of us cannot live with for too long a period of time. In one way or another we will do something about it, either in a constructive or in a destructive fashion. A husband and wife who still talk to each other, who occasionally touch and look at each other but with each feeling gradually more distant from the other, are feeling the loneliness pain that is unique to marriage. To live under the same roof, eat at the same table, sit in the same living room and share the same bed, yet be frightened of love, is torment.

This type of loneliness was vividly portrayed by a housewife who said that whenever she "accidentally" brushed against her husband in the hallway as they passed each other in silence, she was torn between wanting to throw her arms around him and run from him in panic at the same time. Touching served to aggravate her fears to the point of panic. She could not risk loving him for fear of his reaction. To be rejected once more would be the last straw. She could not chance it.

At times all married people have probably known this type

of loneliness. Sitting down to a meal together, your eyes may meet for a brief second or two. To look longer would be to make yourself too vulnerable. Our eyes *do* tell the most about how we feel. Or when you climbed into the family car together, whether for a long trip or a short jaunt down to the corner grocery store, your guarded words only added to the strain that was becoming increasingly intolerable for both of you. You may have seen these moments alone as being a good time to share your feelings and risk "something"—anything at all. But at the same time you were doubly terrified that just such a confrontation might well take place without being sure that you could risk the reaction—if it wasn't what you needed and wanted.

Wanting . . . yet running. That means "walking on eggs" with each other. We can say nothing without first having rehearsed every word in advance. It might offend; it might be the one thing to topple an already teetering relationship. Will he walk out on me if I tell him my hurt? Do I dare to respond to what he said? Will she laugh if I share my sadness now? Will he push me away if I reach out for his hand? Will she use it against me if I express appreciation? Such is the frozen state of loneliness in marriage; two people wanting to risk, but paralyzed at the thought of doing so.

It no longer surprises me that it is frequently the one thing that both persons secretly and desperately want, but each waits for the other to take the first risk.

Marrying a fantasy

"Every man loves two women; the one is the creation of his imagination and the other is yet to be born."[1]

If you plan to marry or have already married, it is certain that you had a preconceived fantasy of your ideal mate or the perfect marriage. After a while, however, you may have begun

[1] #454 Everyman, *Synergisms,* 601 Minnesota Street, San Francisco, California.

to realize that the fantasy to which you were clinging and the person you had chosen were beginning to diverge sharply. At that point one of several things probably happened. You shed your mate. Or, forgetting that only God can make a tree, you embarked on a reform program. You misconstrued the words of the wedding ceremony "And the two shall become one" to mean that your mate should become like you and your fantasy. You would become one in likes, preferences, interests, hobbies, ideas, even reactions and feelings: *yours*. "And the two shall become one" does not indicate which one. The oneness in marriage is not similarity or sameness in matters relating to ideas or feelings but to the oneness of understanding.

Any attempt to mold our mates in an effort to match them to our fantasies is arrogance on our part and an insult to them. It divides, breeds anger, and provokes even greater loneliness.

While it is true that we can never mold or remake another person, we can "allow" them to change. It is our understanding of them that allows them to dare to be what they are today. To insist that your mate conform to your values or likes means that out of fear, he or she may be trying. You may think that he or she is changing, and say to yourself, "You know, I believe it's working." But it is only the outward behavior that is changing. Inside he or she is more frightened of you than ever, and probably very angry, too.

Relinquishing fantasies in marriage is difficult. Our fantasies, based upon what we have been taught and observed since childhood, are sometimes so much a part of us that rather than give them up or modify them, we will end a relationship.

Frequently a new husband or wife will say: "I can't believe it. . . . I found a husband just like my dad . . . and that's what I've always been looking for." "I married a woman who is just the opposite of my mother, and that's what I was looking for."

True. It is impossible to dissociate ourselves from the influence and example of past models, nor do we necessarily have to do so. But in clinging to them too tightly we may not even realize that our selection of a mate is based not upon an appreciation of their individuality, but a belief that we can mold them or force them to change. Two people in marriage will never come to know each other as long as one insists on subtly attempting to mold the other. Never knowing each other, they will feel alienated, defensive and, above all, lonely.

It is our understanding that will, each day, bring forth the person who is being born. In marriage, then, ours is the excitement of having a role in that birth and growth process.

Unfinished business and second guessing

"Unfinished business" is one of the contributing causes to loneliness in marriage. It refers to any unexpressed or unresolved feelings *out of the past*, particularly hurt and anger, that we have experienced but have chosen to stash away, each for his own reason. The trouble is, the moment we attempt to put it under lock and key, it becomes unfinished business for the future. We do not forget "feelings." We may forget the incident itself (the slap, the insult, the neglect), but the feelings that accompanied that incident, that surrounded it, will not evaporate. They have a way of lingering and festering.

If and when we have collected enough unfinished business, we will feel entitled to exchange it for a prize that we have earned; a separation from our mate, divorce, depression, a trip to the hospital, a buying spree, a binge, even homicide or suicide. It all depends upon the type of feelings that we have been collecting.

It isn't surprising that two people with unfinished business become strangers to each other. Neither may be aware of it because the manner in which it is happening is subtle. Each, trying hard to keep the peace at all costs, is afraid to risk offending or irritating. Mistaking an absence of outward conflict for harmony in marriage, each is contending with an increasing amount of residue in the form of unexpressed feelings (otherwise known as garbage).

Not knowing what the other is ever really feeling or thinking, there is second guessing: "I know that you're angry at me. Why don't you just come out and say it?" Second guessers are sometimes correct . . . but not always. That isn't the point. To assume that we *know* what our mates are thinking or feeling without having asked them first is to assert that we know them better than they know themselves. And that will make you all the more frightened of him or her.

When a married couple first comes into my office I stipulate a *contract* in which the important clause is that neither can think or speak for the other. Such statements as "we think" or "she feels" are out. "I think" and "I feel" are in. If one begins to speak for the other I ask that he or she stop and begin again by using "I," not "you." "I am angry because . . .," never "You *make me* angry." In doing this we are assuming responsibility for our own feelings and reactions.

Partners with unfinished business find that the longer it remains unfinished the greater the suspicion, the higher the walls of fear and loneliness. Attempts at second guessing are likely to increase, which only add to the fears and defensiveness of each. While there will be moments of confrontation over disagreement on current issues, rarely can two people deal with matters related to the present if they are still caught up in the past. The point may come when there is such a collection of garbage that they are unable to deal constructively with the present. At that point two people in marriage are totally alienated and each is in the grip of utter loneliness. If there is no understanding whatsoever of present needs and feelings then there is nothing at all.

Dumping

Dumping is the commonest method of dealing with unfinished business within the family. Dumpers are those who unload their previously unexpressed hurts or anger on innocent members of the family who were in no way involved in the initial hurt (or transaction). If Mother has unfinished business with Father, she may provoke ten-year-old Mary into misbehaving in order to unload and dump unexpressed anger on her. Somebody has to get it and Mary seems to be the most likely to take it. In a similar manner, fifteen-year-old Tim, who is angry at his father but afraid to express it for fear of reprisal, may dump on his mother, whom he sees as being willing to take it. Furthermore, if he senses that she is one who will attempt to keep the peace within the family at all costs to herself, she may indeed be a very likely target for dumping by *everyone* within the family.

If individual members of the family cannot deal directly, that is, at the present moment or at an appropriate time in the near future with their unfinished business, then it is possible they are involving innocent members and alienating them as well. In the end the loneliness of everyone will have been compounded.

Parents who make children responsible for their loneliness

When children sense misunderstanding and loneliness between their mother and father, they frequently assume the responsibility for it and punish themselves. One eleven-year-old put it in these terms: "I don't want to risk telling Mother about my hurts because I know that she has enough trouble of her own in just trying to make her hurts understood by Daddy." She was carrying a double burden, her mother's and her own.

Sometimes children feel that because of something they have done or said, they are responsible for a misunderstanding that they see developing between parents. A distraught mother whose increasing fatigue and emotional distress were placing a strain on the relationship with her husband, blurted out to her daughter, "You were a mistake, you know. We had meant to have only five kids." (She was the sixth.) She was placing the responsibility for her loneliness upon this teen-ager.

Though children are sometimes the victims of a power struggle between parents, rarely are they the direct cause of dissension between them. Father: "If you would just behave yourself, Rhonda, you wouldn't cause Mother and me to be so out of sorts with each other." Any attempt to place the responsibility on children for the loneliness that parents feel with each other adds to the loneliness of everyone concerned.

Teen-agers: the loneliness of feeling misunderstood

Because teen-agers feel things intensely, if they are misunderstood it can hurt deeply. "But how can I get my teen-ager to share his feelings with me?" frustrated parents ask. "I take my daughter and son out to dinner alone in hopes that they will talk to me . . . tell me what's bothering them . . . get it off their chest, but it doesn't work." That is because teen-agers choose the time and place to talk and share feelings. They see any attempt to coerce them (by setting up obvious situations) as being a violation of their personhood. The reason that teen-agers do not always share feelings with their parents is not that they are angry at them or even fear being misunderstood. Keeping feelings to themselves at this time in life is sometimes a part of the separation process. As a result they will probably be more willing to share what they feel with their peers than with their parents. But because the mother and father are likely to interpret this as a lack of trust, or losing control, they may continue to pry, alienating their teen-agers even further. Secrets during adolescent and teen-age years are a way of telling big people, "Look, certain things are mine. I don't have to share everything about *me* with *you*." This is as it should be. It contributes to their growing sense of personhood and personal identity. Even in the most intimate of relationships there is selective communication. We may sometimes choose to keep some fantasies and dreams to ourselves. This allows us to maintain our individuality.

Two things add to the situational type of loneliness that teen-agers experience. It is a time in life when the likelihood of being misunderstood is probably greatest of all. Teen-agers are beginning to assume more responsibility for their decisions and feelings. If this is threatening to parents, a power struggle can easily ensue in which parents always have a need to come out the winners. Any confrontation in which the feelings and wisdom of teen-agers are discounted, ignored, or minimized is destructive to the relationship and to the teen-ager. To have our wisdom disregarded, no matter how old we are, is to be hurt at the core of our being. It is also to experience the loneliness of judgment and misunderstanding.

A shortage of strokes also contributes to the loneliness of teen-agers. While they will continue to hug and squeeze little children, they feel awkward in displaying such affection with family members who are older than they are. Similarly, parents may feel awkward in hugging "our big teen-agers." In some families, as the children grow into their teen years, hugging and squeezing give way to horseplay in the form of tickling and wrestling. This is good because, though touching is going on, neither teen-agers nor parents are frightened or feel embarrassed or awkward. Besides, it is almost always fun. And stroking and fun together are an unbeatable combination.

In addition to the decrease of physical attention, teen-agers are frequently discounted in conversations where those in attendance are primarily adults. This, too, aggravates their loneliness. At the age of fourteen or fifteen it is embarrassing to be seen talking to seven- and eight-year-olds, so once again they are caught somewhere in the middle—being unwilling or unable to relate to those younger or older than they are. This is why they need to look for attention outside the home, from peers, through the medium of sports, cheerleading, and positions of leadership in school and the church. Pets for teen-agers (particularly furry cats) provide warm strokes.

Alternatives to loneliness within the family

LISTENING

Nowhere is it more necessary to listen than within the setting of the family. Listening involves not just our ears but every part of our person. Sometimes we hear but we do not listen. We hear the words but are not able or willing to detect the feelings behind the words. If a member of your family is hearing only your words, you are probably both frustrated and lonely. If, on the other hand, he is working to identify with your feelings, then you feel understood. Paul Tournier reminds us: "In order to really understand, we need to listen, not to reply. In order to help anybody open his heart we have to give him time, asking only a few questions as carefully as possible in order to help him better explain his experience. Above all we must not give the impression that we know better than he does what he must do, otherwise we force him to withdraw."[2]

APPRECIATION OF INDIVIDUAL UNIQUENESS

Have you ever noticed that no two leaves on your elm or maple are exactly identical in shape, size, or color? There is always something that distinguishes one from the other. No two snowflakes, roses, or fingerprints are ever alike. Each is a unique entity unto itself.

Similarly, each of us is unique. If you married someone who you felt was just like you, you were only kidding yourself. And even if that were possible, it would be the most boring relationship in the world.

Differentness is particularly threatening within the context of the family. I remember a father, mother, and son who all sat in silence, seemingly unable to relate to one another. Finally the father said of his teen-ager, "Yeah, the boy is just like me, he finds it hard to talk about his feelings too." At that point the son responded for the first time. He jumped out of

[2] Paul Tournier, *To Understand Each Other* (Richmond, Va.: John Knox Press, 1970), p. 25.

his chair and shouted, "For God's sake, Dad, will you please stop trying to make me like you?" I began to get an inkling of what was going on. The father, using power, kept referring to his son as like him. The son in turn felt both angry and frightened; angry at being compared to his father and yet frightened at the prospect of what might happen if he didn't in some way attempt to be what his father thought he should be. Because the father was unwilling to express his feelings, whenever the mother began to risk sharing hers he would shut her off, by a snarl, a grunt, or by interrupting her. He was frightened of his own feelings. Efforts to control the rest of the family were an attempt to avoid having to face his own fear of love. There was no acceptance or appreciation of individual uniqueness in this family.

The fine line between power and authority

Transactional Analysts would say that the *need* of parents to wield power over their children lies within their own inner Prejudiced Archaic Parent.

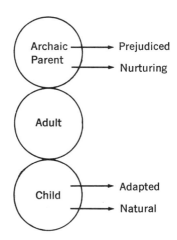

There is a fine line between power and authority. Power is the misuse, the perversion of authority, employed with a *need* to control, win, and be right. Such power most often lies within the Prejudiced Archaic Parent; the nonthinking, programmed, judgmental, and ritualistic ego state.

But power is not only characteristic of the Archaic Prejudiced Parent. It can also slip into the Archaic Nurturing Parent. Though the Archaic Nurturing Parent is concerned about the physical and emotional needs of little people— willing to listen and attempting to understand—it is not always aware of the limits of nurturing or the point at which "Here, let me do it for you" is beginning to render the little person helpless, increasingly dependent, and less willing to exercise his own capabilities. For that reason the Archaic Nurturing Parent often degenerates into a Rescuing Parent, manipulating the child in order to maintain a relationship of dependency.

To illustrate:

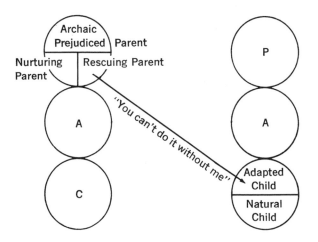

Rescuers, rather than encouraging children to become more responsible for exercising their own inner resources, indirectly discourage such responsibility. It is not uncommon for the Archaic Nurturing Parent to be unable to distinguish between "helping" and "rescuing." "Billy needs my help" may really mean, "Billy can't do it *without me*." There is a difference. If someone points out this need to rescue others, the heated response may be, "You're certainly cold-blooded. Don't you know anything about helping people?" Rescuers find it difficult to see that rescuing is an insult to the rescued; the message being, "On your own you're nothing."

So the pattern of rescuing always does more for the rescuer than for the rescued. It provides him with a needed feeling of power. Keeping others dependent upon him makes him feel more OK, more important, more lovable. But to a little person, persistent rescuing hurts more than a teeth-rattling slap in the face. It's saying: "You're nothing."

The updated P-A-C looks like this:

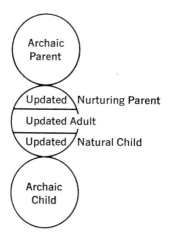

This process of updating goes on for a lifetime. The Adult must always be in a position to evaluate and examine data (top circle), which is the Archaic Nurturing and Prejudiced Parent. Also it must be in a position to be able to evaluate "feeling rackets" in the Archaic Adapted Child (bottom circle).

The healthy Adult ego state (center circle) consists of a happy *coexistence* of all three updated ego states—as they will continue to be for a lifetime.

For our purposes here, because we are evaluating the need for power, the updated Nurturing Parent in the operative Adult is aware of the point at which its nurturing is becoming unhealthy and crippling for children.

Power	*Authority*
(Archaic Parent, Nurturing and Prejudiced)	(Updated Nurturing Parent in the operative Adult)
1. Needs to win. Sees things only in terms of black and white. No grays.	1. No need to win. Interested in what "best fits."
2. Depends on roles; demands respect because of "who I am." Children are not viewed as equals.	2. Children are seen as equals.
3. Makes no provision for the wisdom of children.	3. Puts value on the wisdom of children.
4. Nonthinking position; operates on the basis of prejudice, tradition, and bias.	4. "You think along with me, kids."
5. No admission of humanness; won't apologize; won't show feelings—sadness, tears, hurts—only anger.	5. Can say, "I'm sorry." Not afraid to show feelings.
6. Wins by character assassination; "dumb," "dingbat," "stupid."	6. Respects character—deals only with issues and behavior.

7. Engages in value judgments with personality; good, bad, kind, generous, honest, dishonest, hence setting up levels of expectation for the child to live up to.

7. Never uses such words; praises effort; never evaluates character.

8. *Won't* listen—hears only words, never feelings.

8. Listens—able to identify feelings behind words.

9. Deals with punishment (to win).

9. Deals with discipline. Sets limits in advance on behavior and enforces them with firmness.

10. Always speaks for the child; "We don't do that Billy, do we?"

10. Allows child to speak for himself.

Constructive expression of resentments and appreciations

Rather than using the word anger I prefer to use the word resentment. When two people care for each other there will be times of resentment. The fact that we do occasionally react this way to those for whom we care is *proof* of the fact that we care. Very early in the course of counseling married couples I ask each to risk an expression of what they resent and appreciate about each other. It is good to mix the two together.

The ground rules are that when one is talking the other cannot respond or in any way defend himself or herself until afterward. Listening is what we are after. After both have given full expression to resentment and appreciation they are asked to restate not only what they thought the other said but also *felt*; not merely to parrot back words but to reflect feelings. Such a summary lets the other know that there is understanding. Once there is that, then there is relaxation, defenses go down, and the two may proceed into an intellectual discussion centering on their disagreement.

But if it is difficult and frightening for couples to express what they resent about each other it is even more difficult for them to express appreciation. There are two reasons for this. One is that if there is unfinished business they will find it difficult if not impossible to deal with appreciation at the moment. Secondly, we frequently find it difficult to express appreciation because of our fear of love; fear of embarrassment, clumsiness, awkwardness, crying. An expression of appreciation of little things means a great deal. One wife expressed it well when she said that her husband, with astonishing regularity, thanked her for the way in which she neatly pressed and then folded his handkerchiefs, placing them in his drawer, for her thoughtfulness in seeing to it that he had clean towels on his rack in the bathroom, and buttering his toast for breakfast.

In the initial phases of counseling, one partner will attempt to make the other feel responsible for the lack of communication. "She makes me mad" or "He is always trying to hurt me" are common charges. When that happens they are asked again to rephrase these resentments more responsibly, beginning with "I."

Note the progression downward in terms of gradually assuming personal responsibility for our own reaction.

"You're an insulting person."

"You insulted me."

"That's an insult."

"I feel insulted."

"I hurt."

On the bottom rung we have assumed full responsibility for our reaction to what was said, in no way blaming the other for our response. Making others responsible for our reaction places them immediately on the defensive and from that moment on all hope of meaningful communication is lost. If each is sincerely working to understand the other, there is no manipulation in which one is placed in the position of having to defend or justify what he or she said.

A popular comedienne said that she and her husband resolved that neither would ever go to sleep at night without first expressing any resentment that either one might be harboring. "At this point," she said glumly, "neither of us has gotten any sleep for three weeks." Well, it's humorous, but if we know what it is that makes our mate react with anger then we are becoming acquainted with a very important part of his person.

Appropriate times for sharing

The wife of a prominent civic leader told of the time that she and her husband were on their way to a very important function at the country club. Upon getting out of the car, he sized her up from head to foot, then blurted out, "Honey, that dress is simply too short for an occasion like this." Granted, he may have been honest in his reaction but it was simply the wrong time for such sharing. It would have been better if he had noticed and said something when they were getting ready to go out.

In a relationship that is characterized by understanding there is an awareness of the readiness of the other to give and take at *that particular moment*. Even if he had thought to himself that his wife's dress was too short, it would have been better if he had thought it *to himself* when they arrived at the club.

The limits of intimacy

We have dealt at length in this book with the importance of risks and the sharing of our feelings. But there are limits to intimacy. In a day and age when the emphasis is on "coming on straight," honesty can be a form of cruelty, a way to rid oneself of guilt. Must a wife confess to the man she is about to marry all her sexual exploits with previous suitors? It may leaven her guilt but at the expense of losing his trust . . . even the relationship itself. It is possible that such honesty is veiling a message: "You just don't measure up to so-and-so." Confession is sometimes underlined by anger.

People may use frank communication as a means of attacking each other. To continually reveal that which *we know* will hurt is a way of punishing the person you love. Total honesty may also be a form of emotional blackmail implying, "If I tell you everything about me then this obligates you to tell me everything about you."

There is such a thing then as selective communication. Though honesty is important in marriage and family, there does not have to be a childlike obligation to report everything. There will be times when we have the courage to say, "Please, stop, I don't want to hear about that."

10 the aloneness and loneliness of the aged

"It's hard to grow older gracefully." The speaker was not someone in retirement but a man forty-seven years of age, not old as we think of as old. But, like the rest of us, he is growing older.

"No one should live beyond seventy," one white-thatched gentleman reflected. "If a man can't do in seventy years what he wants to do he is not going to have much chance after seventy to do it."

But it is a matter of individual opinion, attitude, and life-style.

"Every day," said a seventy-six-year-old bejeweled woman, dressed in a bright red outfit that somehow seemed to reflect her infectious optimism, "I find something good—something new in life. I always have, and I still do. If I felt sad I wouldn't last long." Slowly surveying the sunny sitting room of the convalescent home in which we were chatting, she continued, "Do you see those women? Every day I try to get them to dress up, wear jewelry, put on their best clothes and some make-up, and get them out of their bathrobes and slippers. After all, life isn't over."

Clearly, the aged person is what he always has been, only more so. If we have said "yes" to life in earlier years, were flexible, fluid, open to change, and adjusted well to disappointment, setbacks, and losses, it is likely that we will age with the same attitude. But if our attitude has been a blatant "no" to life, putting our utmost efforts and energies into flailing out against it, it means that there has been a rigidity and unwillingness to bend with the natural flow of events. In all likelihood it is with this same attitude that we will age, only more so.

Hans Selye has placed in correct perspective the place of stress. He defines stress as wear and tear on the body, indicating that there is a close tie-in between aging and stress. Using the term "adaptive energy," he notes that each of us inherits a certain amount of adaptive energy and that nothing can be added to it. The rate at which we use it up determines our aging process.

Stressing that many nervous and emotional disturbances are related to the speed of self-consumption or the rate at which our adaptive energy is depleted, he says that our true age is dependent upon the ravages of time.

Among all my autopsies (and I have performed quite a few) I have never seen a man who died of old age. In fact I do not think anyone has ever died of old age yet. . . . To die of old age would mean that all of the organs of the body would be worn out proportionately, merely by having been used too long. This is never the case. We invariably die because one vital part has worn out too early in proportion to the rest of the body. . . . There is always one part which wears out first and wrecks the whole human machinery merely because the other parts cannot function without it.[1]

His theory makes sense. The secret would seem to lie in our willingness and ability to grow old gracefully. A set life-style makes no allowance for change, spontaneity, flexibility, or variety; hence greater stress. If we cannot bend or consider and

[1] Hans Selye, *The Stress of Life* (New York: McGraw-Hill, 1956), p. 276.

evaluate new ideas, methods, findings, and formulas in the light of change and discovery, that type of rigidity affects the aging process.

The aged and "a stroke vacuum"

It would be impossible to estimate the percentage of the aged in the population who are simply forgotten, but it is large. They are shunted aside for no tangible reason, certainly not because family or society is intentionally cruel. No, just forgotten, abandoned and, dare I say it, discarded like refrigerators or automobiles that have outlived their usefulness and purpose.

In a small coastal village, living in a house that was close enough to the sea so that its sounds penetrated the walls twenty-four hours a day, was a retired fisherman who was crippled with arthritis but obviously hurting more because of the pain of his aloneness than from his ailment. The shades were pulled and a twelve-inch black-and-white television set— obviously in need of repair—was his only company. As the former captain of a seagoing fishing boat, his face reflected fifty years of daily exposure to the salt air and sun. In a voice barely audible he said, "Born and raised here—lived here all my life. Used to be that old fishing buddies dropped around, or a minister or two. No more. Don't know what's happened . . . just forgotten, I guess."

Not all of the aged will risk saying that, but many feel it: FORGOTTEN.

But sometimes it isn't only that the aged are forgotten by persons in close proximity. Sometimes, because of the actual situation of the aged, sources of attention can be practically nil. Children are frequently far away, mates are in poor health, incapacitated, or dead—as are many former close friends and past associates. Poor health is apt to restrict the mobility that would allow the aged to move about freely to seek companionship. In the case of men, retirement at sixty-five suddenly vaults them into the predicament of being cut off from the intimate associations that they have known with others on a day-in and day-out basis. The symptoms of their lonely pain may be characterized as despair. It *is* possible to die of a broken heart and hearts may break when all *former* sources of attention and love are gone.

But for others, it is not that hopeless. Some never give up on love. Without their long-standing sources of love and strokes, they turn to other methods of stroke procurement. Letter-writing, for example. "This past Christmas I wrote seventy personal messages on the Christmas cards that I mailed out to old friends and relatives," recalled one seventy-eight-year-old woman. A widow, each day she spends two or three hours answering a never-ending small mountain of mail that is stuffed daily into her all-too-small mailbox. Not only is her letter-writing providing her with a method of stroke procurement, but it is also a way of filling otherwise empty hours.

Some of the aged also find greater delight in the attention of children. Those with grandchildren are often heaped with generous portions of strokes, though their tolerance level to the shouting, fighting, and general racket that accompany such stroking, is low. In other words, there comes the moment when noisy playing begins to outweigh the value of the strokes that they are receiving.

Not everyone will achieve the fame of a Grandma Moses, but the vigor and enthusiasm with which she took up painting when old caught the attention of the world. We're talking now about self strokes. Many of the aged surprise themselves, when in trying some new things, they tap resources within themselves that they did not know were there.

No matter how old people get there is always something new that they can try, experiment with, explore, for the *first time:* wood-carving, rock-hunting, taking piano lessons, raising flowers or, as in the case of a burly former wrestler, now retired, sculpting with clay. Our new ways of passing time (and stroking ourselves) may amuse friends and neighbors, even cause raised eyebrows. After all, it might seem out of character for an embattled former wrestler to turn to sculpture.

One aspect of the trauma of retirement is: "Now what do I do with myself until—" For those who are physically able, *volunteer work* in local hospitals, churches, and other institutions is one answer. "I'll do anything at all to feel as if I'm still of some use to society," reports a retired nurse. Whereas before she was head nurse on the day shift at the local hospital, now she is working for nothing in the same hospital, cheerfully wheeling a cart laden with reading material from room to room.

Dow Coffman, manager of Hearthstone Manor in Folsom, California, a retirement center, classifies the home as "an accumulation of memories." *Pastimes,* as we mentioned earlier, are another option that we have, and will probably become more important for the aged. Whether on a park bench in the inner-city with a friend, or in a retirement home in the suburbs, various forms of "remember when" may be engaged in.

Aging and the loss of our identity

In a phenomenon that defies understanding, aging is also accompanied by the gradual loss of our identity; somehow it is taken from us, our personhood gives way to classification. We become one of the old folks, old timers, or senior citizens. The aged deeply resent this. One hale and hearty new resident of a retirement center recapped a seemingly typical experience like this: "On the first Sunday after I had taken up residency at the center, I attended a local church for the first time. Afterward someone extended me her hand and said sweetly, 'Welcome. You must be from the old folks' home down the road.'

It was, she related, her first experience of trauma in retirement. To be called by our name, even if we live to be one hundred, is to be reminded of our distinct and unique individuality.

It is true that we treat the aged as though they were either nonentities or, as one sprightly gentleman complained, with a type of gentleness that borders on the gooey side; much in the same fashion with which we coddle little kids.

Her grandson probably means well when he greets "Grandma" with "Please don't bother to get up—just sit where you are." But "Grandma" may not only be able to get up to greet her nephew (who at twenty-five is fifty pounds overweight), she may also be able to best him in a walking marathon. The aging appreciate being treated just like everyone else, with no special concern expressed because they are old.

Aging and the loss of independence

Aging is not only accompanied by an increasing frequency of actual losses but also the fear of anticipated losses. One of our most upsetting fears centers on the gradual realization that our bodies are losing their vitality. When muscles first begin to soften and body tone and chemistry begin to diminish, the prospect of losing our independence is apt to throw us into ever-mounting despair. At the point where failing reflexes, eyesight, or hearing demand that we give up driving and sell our automobile, another aspect of independence is lost.

One day an eighty-six-year-old man, with the fierce pride of a teen-ager, showed me what he obviously felt was one of his last prized possessions, his driver's license. Even though he had not driven a car for many years he refused to throw his license away. He was still carrying it in his billfold encased in plastic. For him it symbolized an aspect of an independence that he once knew and was still desperately hanging on to, even though it was now but a symbol.

For the aging, at the point where hope flickers, the will to live dies. "It's too bad I have to get so old," a chain-smoking, wheelchair-bound man sadly commented. "All I have to look forward to is the ability to walk again." It didn't sound much like something to look forward to, but it was *something*.

Another woman that I talked to in a convalescent home said that she had lost her last hope in the long struggle to maintain some semblance of independence after she fell and broke her hip. Now she was dependent upon her son for everything. For one who had always lived a rigorous life, enjoyed good health and independence, such a status had resulted in the loss of all incentive to live.

Aging—and our ultimate aloneness

With aging, the reality of our individual aloneness is brought more sharply into focus. "We marry two by two, but we die one by one." In younger years, with their accompanying vitality, the presence of children, and the promise of a bright future ahead, the prospect of our ultimate aloneness seems mighty remote. But the compounding losses that accompany the aging process force us in one way or another to deal with that reality. Those fears crystallize at the time our mate dies. No matter how well prepared we think we are for that moment there is no escaping the trauma and grief that accompany a realization of the fact that we are indeed alone.

A seventy-five-year-old woman whose husband of forty-five years had died, said that her most painful hours were between five and seven each evening; a time that she had spent with her husband, eating and discussing the events of the day. It did not help to see other men walking past her house, headed for home and their wives, at suppertime. Her stark aloneness was the most vivid to her then. In addition, birthdays and anniversaries were other difficult times for her—what with many memories and feelings becoming so much more alive.

The more we invest of ourselves in someone else, and they

in us, the more intense are our feelings of aloneness and grief when we are separated through death. When someone understands us they absorb a part of us. They are able to feel what we feel to the point of actually assimilating it into their person. We become alive *in* them; and they become alive *in* us. This is the "oneness" of understanding. There are no limits as to the degree of understanding that two people can attain in a relationship. The longer "we absorb each other," the more we become one. Physical unity is always secondary to the unity of understanding.

When death separates us, the deceased take part of us along with them to the grave. Our sense of loss is therefore twofold. We are separated from the one that we love for his or her unique personhood; but we are also suddenly separated from a part of us that we invested in them. This is what is meant when someone says "a part of me died when my wife died." We more deeply mourn the loss of those in whom we have invested more of ourselves. It is most often in our mates that we have made the greatest investment. For this reason the grief of aloneness in the elderly is worse when their mates die. Their investment has been greater.

At the time of death what we absorbed from them in memories and feelings also becomes more vivid. While there is a sadness in realizing that there will never again live another like the one who is dead, there is at the same time a feeling of gladness. The uniqueness of the other is more fully appreciated now. While there may have been a gradual realization of this during the years spent together, that appreciation will suddenly take on new dimensions. Whenever we say, "There will never be another like him or her," we are expressing both a sadness and a gladness. This makes allowance for two things: (a) it helps us to recall the loved one with even greater appreciation; (b) it permits us to love others knowing that it could never be with the same quality or intensity of love. For that reason, we will not be betraying the one who is dead.

An energetic eighty-year-old widow may have expressed

the sentiments of many of the aging when, in referring to marriage, she said, "I believe that everyone loves *deeply* only once in a lifetime." Pressed to elaborate, she went on to say that when she lost her husband it was not that she was *incapable* of loving a possible suitor as deeply again, but that she was *reluctant* to. If our investment in a mate has been total and complete over a number of years, a type of reverence may surround the relationship. In the case of this vibrant and alert woman, the reasons for her reluctance to love deeply again are not important. Hers was a responsible choice. She still cared about people, though not with the investment that she had made with one. She was not lonely.

It happens that our loyalty and devotion to the deceased may prompt us to feel that we are betraying that love if we dare to love again in the future—if there are possibilities for love. As stated in a previous chapter, if we choose not to love again and if we can be responsible for the consequences of that choice then it is a responsible one. But if we are reluctant to reach out for love again, then our loneliness is of our own doing. Others can never *replace* a loved one. But they can help, each in his own unique way, to fill a need that we have as long as we live, to love and be loved.

Childlike versus childish—fun and aging

With aging there may be a laying aside of those qualities that are *childish* (sulkiness, self-centeredness, dependence, and irresponsibility), but there does not need to be a loss of the qualities that are *childlike* (spontaneity, inquisitiveness, and curiosity). The manner in which we allow ourselves to continue exercising these characteristics determines the spirit with which we age.

It's true; we are conceived in a moment of profound fun. Born out of fun, we are born into it. Each squirm, sniff, gape, and kick ignites some new fresh sensation within us. Incomprehensible sounds storm around us: cooings, scrapings, squeakings. Hourly new things come into focus. Fun is simply in being.

As the child grows he makes the most out of what is at hand, whether it is a hairpin or a gum wrapper. Children have the imagination to transform the gum wrapper into a baby blanket or a hairpin into a baby. As the child pretends, he allows that which is within him to flow, oblivious to what other people think or feel about the silliness of it all. The child is whole, trusting in his own inner resources. He can do crazy things on impulse, feeling no compulsion to continue an activity beyond the moment it ceases to give him pleasure. He is ready for a new adventure at any time. But with aging, the Natural Child in us is apt to be blocked out by the "Compliant" or Adapted Child. As our fears of being unlovable compound, we begin to stop playing in the way others do not approve of.

A number of parental injunctions, verbal and nonverbal hasten this change.

1. "You are most important to me when you're *doing*, not simply *being*." Work becomes more important than play. It isn't that work is not important; it is that it becomes *more* important. We all need to play for at least an hour and a half each weekday, and two hours on weekends. There must be a happy coexistence between work and play if we are to stay in touch with our Natural Child.

2. "Anything worth doing is worth doing well." Instead of allowing ourselves simply to "feel" and enjoy our fun, we concentrate on perfecting it, contributing even further to our stress. We don't need reasons to have fun. There doesn't have to be a purpose behind it. With almost everything else we do in life there has to be a purpose: at school, home, church, or work. Not so with fun.

Some of us consider jogging and exercise to be fun. Yet when jogging, if we are concentrating on bettering yesterday's time, we may be more aware of the second hand on our wristwatch than the warmth of the sun on our face, or the sound of the birds overhead. If body conditioning is the by-product of our fun then it is good. But if body conditioning is uppermost in our minds then it is slightly less fun. "I've got to get fifty push-ups in before breakfast even though I am ten minutes late for work right now."

I disagree with those who say "my work is fun." Work always entails a certain amount of planning, programming, scheduling, stress, and purpose. Work may be enjoyable and rewarding, but a good portion of the "fun" of fun lies in our ability to put aside programming, and do whatever feels the best to us.

With P-A-C, we speak of fun as being those times that we "let the kid out," our inner kid. But it isn't just a matter of letting our kid go. Unless our Adult is *aware* of the limits to which our kid can extend itself, it is possible that the kid may run wild, overextend itself, and then feel guilty, depressed, and play "kick me." If we are just learning how to have fun again, after having forgotten how, we may let the kid out too far. Afterward, kicking ourselves because we spent too much money, or took too much time away from the job, or had our first extramarital affair, our "guilt" may have the effect of crippling us for a while. Our Adult then is aware of the extent to which our Natural Child can extend itself *today*.

3. "It is important to win." If fun becomes competitive, with a need to win, then there is never an escape from the very thing that often unnerves us in our day-to-day work world, competitiveness and manipulation. One five-year-old asked her mother to play a new game with her and then confessed, "Mom, I don't know how to play this game, but I'll find a way." She did. A need to win takes the fun out of fun. If we are in the I'M OK—YOU'RE NOT OK position it is likely that we will have a need to win. Even with fun we will have to control others.

4. "Fun is something that is pursued; it is found elsewhere." This is the misconception that leads us to think that in order

to have fun we must go across town, across country, or across the ocean. Fun is in being alive to what is going on around us at the moment with accompanying ability to respond to it.

Many people will say that their most miserable vacations have been those in which they have driven three thousand miles in less than two weeks in a car with no air conditioning across deserts where the temperature hovered consistently around 100 degrees in order to get to camp grounds where the tents were spaced fifteen feet apart.

A substantial number of today's public have given up the frantic pace in which a month's sightseeing is compressed into one week. Bill Emerson, writing in the old *Saturday Evening Post*, commented on the sort of fun that our jet age is returning to. "When a person goes back to the bicycle . . . dogs become dogs again . . . and snap at your raincoat; potholes become personal and getting there is all the fun."

Consistent with our idea that fun is something that must be pursued elsewhere is the belief that "fun is in being entertained." With aging we are apt to be afflicted with "spectatoritis"; in the bleachers, but rarely down on the field. Having fun can easily mean the satisfaction of taking in commodities, fights, food, drink, cigarettes, people, lectures, movies, and books. They are all swallowed. The world can become one big object for our appetite, a big apple, a big breast. The highest paid people in America, and the world, are those who entertain us. We are willing to dole out large sums of money in order to be entertained.

As we get older we need continually to update our Natural Child. One way of doing this is to write out a fun list.

25 ways in which you had fun as a child
10 free ways in which you have fun today
10 expensive ways in which you have fun today
10 ways in which you have fun alone
10 ways in which you have fun with people

I have kept a number of fun lists that my patients have given to me. Here are some of the things that they did for fun as children. Bring back any memories?

Playing with dough Mother had left over
Walking in a warm summer rain
Putting cards on my bike wheels to make a noise
Walking with smashed cans on our shoes
Sitting in a tree listening to the leaves rustle
Being buried in leaves
Riding on a piece of cardboard down a snow-covered hill
Playing "kick the can" after dark
Watching the tiny crabs in the tide pools
Swinging from a rope in a tree into the swimming hole
Swimming under water with eyes open
Watching a bird's nest
Sucking on icicles
Spending two cents at the candy store
Playing poison on the way to the store, never stepping in a
    square with a design on it
Never stepping on ants on the sidewalk unless you wanted it
    to rain
Playing hide and seek in the corn fields just before dark
Fishing at night on the lake
Flying kites
Playing in the attic on a rainy day, going through old trunks
Watching a sow have a litter of piglets, the first birds and bees
    lesson
Walking the railroad ties; looking for old spikes as the black-
    smith paid two cents apiece for them
Skipping stones on the lake
Having a doll funeral under the trees
Drinking warm milk in the milk house right after milking
Racing under the clothes blowing in the wind on the clothes line
Opening doors
Jumping ditches
Getting dirty after a bath
Talking to the animals in the zoo

Going to the mailbox
Running through the sprinkler
Walking barefoot through leaves in the fall

Recalling the fun that we had as children is the first step in tapping the resources of our Natural Child. There are some adults who are still young enough to enjoy doing some of the crazy things they did when they were kids: walking the railroad ties, skipping stones on the lake, watching birds' nests, and so on. Grownups who are still able to find ways of having fun in this fashion may be aging in years but they are not aging in spirit.

Because aging is frequently accompanied by loss of agility and stamina, the nature of our fun will have to alter somewhat. We may no longer be able to jump ditches or walk the railroad ties, but there are many things that we can continue to do.

Adult "spectator-itis" fun usually involves spending money:

Eating out
Going to the theater
Entertaining friends
Water skiing
Golf
Target shooting
Loading ammunition
Camping
Drinking
Going to nightclubs
Buying a new suit or dress
Attending concerts
Redecorating a room or the house
Having hair done at the beauty parlor
Bowling
Buying jewelry

Any type of activity in which we are not exercising our natural resources may give us "pleasure," but it isn't fun in the sense that we are utilizing our own creativity and spontaneity.

Here are some of the things that adults do for fun, alone (most of which are free):

Take a warm bath
Write letters
Go for a walk
Daydream
Lie in the sun
Watch people at concerts
Walk in the rain
Watch TV in bed
Think
Draw blueprint for dream houses
Look at old snapshots
Watch the river
Work puzzles
Enjoy smells in the woods
Whistle
Clean the junk drawer
Play with dogs and cats
Read the want ads
Try to figure out how I can live if I retire
Nonprofessional reading
Plan "if I had money" trips
Read newspapers from other cities
Watch the seasons change
Make long-distance phone calls
Sit in front of the fireplace with the lights out
Walk on the beach
Take coffee breaks
Meet new people
Hold small babies
Eat ice-cream cones
Ride cable cars
Laugh
Send funny postcards to friends
Sleep late

Satirize TV commercials
Talk to myself
Watch and listen to a storm
Listen to sound of rain on the roof

As long as we live we can have fun. It is only the nature of our toys that will change.

We read that it is wise to begin preparing for retirement early, at forty-five. But preparing for retirement is more than a plan—monetarily or otherwise—that we devise at a given age and work toward. It is a life-style, an attitude, the art of growing older *gracefully*.

11 loneliness and religion

With something bordering on pride, most of us think of ourselves as religious or nonreligious. The feeling of pride is based on an amalgam of things.

"But everybody is religious." As religion and politics continue to be two subjects in life that ignite our most heated discussions, that flat assertion could very well raise your dander. But it is probable that if you take pride in thinking of yourself as religious, you may break out in a wide smile and use it as added ammunition on a friend or neighbor who snickers at devout people ("They're the worst hypocrites of all") and organized religion ("All the church wants is people's money").

Trying to get two people to agree on a single definition of religion is about as difficult as trying to get them to agree on the World Series winner before the baseball season gets under way in the spring. It's impossible. For that reason this chapter may, for some, raise more questions than it answers.

Not surprisingly, then, our definitions of religion are wide and varied, if not sometimes judgmental. More often than not our inability to agree results in a game of "Mine is better than yours." Played with a good deal of gusto and flourish between religious and nonreligious people, the game revolves around the idea that life is a kind of competition in being good: "I'm just as good as Charley, who calls himself a Christian and goes to church every Sunday."

Another group views religion as adherence to approved rituals: "Ted and Alice are so religious. Have you noticed they always say grace before meals?"

Yet others hold fast to the idea that religion is a vast assortment of don'ts: "Ralph is the most religious person I know. He never drinks, cusses, or gambles." To which nonreligious people respond, "What in the world *does* Ralph do, anything?"

Though I am never quite sure what someone means when he says, frequently through clenched teeth, "No more of that religion stuff for me; I got too much of it shoved down my throat when I was a kid," his current gagging probably came about because, in the name of religion, well-meaning parents enforced a rigid code of do's and don'ts on him.

A good deal of competition is played out between organized religions throughout the world: "Mine is better than yours," "We're going to heaven and you're not," or "But Mr. Calhoun, how can you say that the Buddhists are religious *too*?"

Religion? An illusion, scoffed Freud. He compared it to "obsessional neuroses" found in children, "having its origin in man's helplessness in confronting the forces of nature outside and the instinctive forces within himself."[1]

Because the child cannot use his reason, he controls and represses his inquisitiveness by the use of certain emotional forces and develops what Freud refers to as an "illusion." As an adult, when confronted by the same dangerous, uncontrollable and un-understandable forces within and outside himself, he remembers and "regresses to an experience he had as a child when he felt protected by a father whom he thought

[1] Quoted in Erich Fromm, *Psychoanalysis and Religion* (New Haven and London: Yale University Press, 1950), p. 10.

to be of superior wisdom and strength, and whose love and protection he should win by obeying his commands and avoiding transgressions of his prohibitions."[2] It is not surprising, then, that Freud passed religion off as an illusion; something that man must relinquish if he is to face up to his aloneness and insignificance in the world.

But Erich Fromm asks, "Which kind of religion?"

There is no one without a religious need, a need to have a frame of orientation and an object of devotion; but this statement does not tell us anything about a specific content in which this religious need is manifest. Man may worship animals, trees, idols of gold or stone, an invisible god, a saintly man or diabolic leaders; he may worship his ancestors, his nation, his class or party, money or success; his religion may be conducive to the development of destructiveness or of love, of domination or of brotherliness.[3]

Is there any common ground at all upon which we can proceed?

I would like to suggest that religion is the *sum total* of the direction that our individual efforts take us in assuming responsibility for the two basic conditions of our existence: our ultimate aloneness and our loneliness. The word religion itself is taken from the Latin word *religare* which means "to bind together." Assuming responsibility for both our aloneness and loneliness is nothing more than searching for answers to the "how" and "why" of our involvement with the universe and with each other. That search begins when we are small, takes different directions, and finds expressions in different modes and objects of worship. This makes us all religious. How religious we become depends upon how vigorously we pursue and discover answers that satisfy us, and fulfill our needs.

Among the many things that we experience in our aloneness is a type of discontent, the nature of which seeks an ever-expanding framework of orientation to the whole of existence.

[2] *Ibid,* p. 11.
[3] *Ibid,* p. 25.

While it is true that animals are happy as long as they have enough to eat and good health, we are not satisfied with that. "Man is the only animal that can be bored, that can be discontented, that can feel evicted from paradise. Man is the only animal for whom his own existence is a problem which he has to solve and from which he cannot escape."[4] Nietzsche echoes this: "He who has a 'why' to live can bear with almost any 'how.' "[5]

Viktor Frankl, in citing the necessity of satisfying the "why" of life, notes the instance of two fellow prisoners who were behind barbed wire with him during World War II. Both, contemplating suicide, could no longer find any reason to go on living. But in conversation with Frankl each came to the realization that he had a semblance of responsibility in the future; one to a child who was waiting for him in a foreign country; the other to a series of books that were yet to be finished.

"The man who becomes conscious of the responsibility he bears toward a human being who affectionately waits for him, or to an unfinished work, will never be able to throw away his life."[6]

At the heart of our discontent then, is a need for confirmation of our OK-ness by people, but reaching even beyond in order to determine whether or not our individual existence is of any purpose or value in relation to the overall cosmic process itself—a type of I'M OK—YOU'RE OK within the framework of the universe itself.

The nature of our discontent

The discontent of persons in their aloneness is experienced in two ways, beginning when they are little.

[4] *Ibid*, p. 23.
[5] Viktor Frankl, *Man's Search for Meaning* (Boston: Beacon Press, 1963).
[6] *Ibid*, p. 126.

What is the world?
Who made it?
What causes the seasons?
Why doesn't the ocean freeze?
Do animals talk to each other?
How can a fly walk on the ceiling without
falling off?
Why does a cow keep chewing when it isn't
eating?

These questions all center on the "how" of creation:

How am *I* involved in the world?
How come little brother gets to go to the store
with Dad more often than I do?
When it thunders does it mean that God is mad
at *me*?
Why do snakes stare at *me*?
Do *I* get warts from toads?
Why does the sun burn *my* skin?
How come *I'm* afraid of Jane?

Here, curiosity flows out of a framework in which the *I* is
at the center. It not only asks "What is the world?"; it also
asks "What value if any, is my existence—in relation to all of
it?" While our search for answers to the "why" of our involvement is carried out for the purpose of establishing the manner
in which we are related to the overall whole, it is never with
a wish to be absorbed in it; rather to continually enhance our
sense of individual uniqueness and worth in relation to it.

Every living thing becomes our brother and sister: plant,
insect, animal, and person. Whether it is a cup of cold water
given to a thirsty hobo, the diligence with which the school
custodian sweeps the floors and washes classroom black-
boards, the faithfulness of a boy in feeding his dog, or the
tenderness of a little girl nursing a bird with a broken wing
back to health, every act is seen as having some worth in relation to what Alan Watts refers to as the "endless knot of

nature"[7]—that is, the interrelatedness of all living things.

In all civilizations it is unmistakably clear that in seeking answers to the "why" of our involvement, man has never had a clear picture of his place or role in the universe. Fear has played a major role in the development of religions (fear of forces of nature, earthquakes, floods, hurricanes, etc.), and the strongest fear has been the fear of death. But Joseph Gaer reminds us that the dominant belief has always been that *life has purpose*. Hence, the "why" at the center of our discontent. "In keeping with this belief men everywhere have established codes of behavior and clothed themselves in appropriate ritualism and creeds which differ from one another in practice though they are similar in theory, particularly at their starting point. And commandments were formulated to keep the believers in harmony with and dedicated to their basic concepts of life's purposes."[8]

We cannot tolerate the thought of a purposeless existence in a purposeless world.

Isn't this what we mean when we say, "I feel at home with you," or "I feel at home in this place"? To say that we feel at home with someone means that we, in some manner, feel that our lives are touching, interweaving, interdependent. It isn't uncommon for us to travel great distances in order to be with someone with whom we feel at home.

Abusing the "how"

In our quest to understand the "how" of the universe there is always the danger of overextending the application of our reason, and this we have done.

In the process of wanting to understand the universe, we

[7] Alan Watts, *Nature, Man and Woman* (New York: Vintage Books, 1970), p. 10.
[8] Joseph Gaer, *What the Great Religions Believe* (New York: Dodd, Mead and Co., 1963).

have tried to control and dissect it from without, interfering with its natural wisdom from within. Forgetting that the highest purpose of nature is simply to exist, nothing more and nothing less, we have taken to probing into it with instruments. Alan Watts, for one, believes that because science has insisted on studying nature piecemeal, the end result has been that we have come to view the control of the universe in the same fashion—piecemeal. He warns that if our primary preoccupation is with rigid and minute classification of nature into species, whether "birds or fish, chemicals or bacilli," science becomes technology and "men start to extend their control of the world."[9]

He goes on:

The scientist *as* scientist does not see nature at all, or rather he sees it only by means of an instrument of measurement, as if trees became visible to the carpenter only as he sawed them into planks or marked them out with his ruler. More importantly, man as *ego* does not see nature at all. For man as ego is man identifying himself or his mind, his total awareness, with the narrowed and exclusive style of attention which we call consciousness.[10]

The phenomenon of wonder

Though little persons, and big ones, too, want answers as to the "how" of creation to satisfy their intellectual curiosity, there is a point at which they seem to prefer that the unknown be left alone, not needing to understand it.

Even though a father might do a good job of explaining to children the "how" of the California poppy, particularly the manner in which it folds up its petals in the evening as if to say good night to the world, the child at times simply wants to sit alone, to go blank intellectually and experience the phenomenon of this wonder.

There is beauty in mystery, in the unknown. A teen-ager,

[9] Watts, *Nature, Man and Woman*, p. 60.
[10] *Ibid*, p. 66.

reflecting on the phenomenon of wonder, as Voltaire did before him, said, "If there were not a God, I would have to invent one." God, taking many forms and assuming many names, is frequently a by-product of this phenomenon of wonder.

We fail to see the difference between fear of the unknown and respect for the unknown. "The courageous are not only those who probe the unknown but know at what point to simply respect it."[11]

A grandfather who is able to experience a sense of wonder with his grandchildren as together they examine the mysterious movements of a furry caterpillar, has retained a necessary ingredient of his personhood. The same grandfather, once he understands all about the sun, the atmosphere, and the rotation of the earth, will still be able to experience a sense of wonder at the phenomenon of the sunset itself.

There is wisdom in knowing when to respect the unknown by going blank in order that we might experience the concreteness of a thing in its actuality. This does not mean that we grow intellectually lazy or stop thinking; rather we know the point at which our intellectualization would do well to concede to our need of experiencing a sense of wonder in the face of the unknown.

Albert Schweitzer coined the term "invisible barriers" to describe the point at which it is unwise to probe beyond:

The more we try to see the development of things in each field whatever, the more we become conscious that to each epoch there are certain limits of knowledge before which it has to come to a halt and always at the very moment when it was apparently bound to advance to a higher and definitive knowledge that seemed just within its grasp. The real history of progress in physics, philosophy and religion, and more especially in psychology, is the history of incomprehensible cessations of conceptions that were unattainable by a given epoch, in spite of all that happened to lead up to them— of the thoughts it did not think, not because it could not, but be-

[11] *Ibid*, p. 83.

cause there was some mysterious command upon it not to. In the same way, the true history of art is the history of invisible, insuperable barriers, which only fall when the due time comes, without anyone understanding why this happens exactly when it happens, and not just as well earlier or later.[12]

A high degree of the excitement that man and wife feel in anticipating the birth of a baby lies in the very mystery of the pregnancy experience itself. While it may be fun to guess the sex of the baby, it is unfortunate if the experience itself is only one of probing and intellectualizing. Measuring the heartbeat ("If it is a girl the heartbeat is supposed to be slower"), checking its size in the womb ("If it is a boy it will be bigger"), the time of conception ("At particular times of the month there is greater likelihood that conception will result in a boy"), may overshadow a simple sense of wonder at the phenomenon of pregnancy. I, for one, will be sad when the day comes (and it will) when science is able to predict the sex of a baby accurately.

It isn't surprising, then, that our fears related to the manner in which we worry about tomorrow make us miserable today. Tomorrow *must* always remain a mystery. The moment we try to unlock its door, outlining what could happen or certainly will happen, not only do we become anxious but our preoccupation with what lies ahead contaminates our awareness (Adult) of beauty and pleasure now.

But don't we need to plan for tomorrow, to think ahead? Only if in our planning we make allowance for the mystery of tomorrow's unfolding in the manner in which it is going to unfold. This could mean that sickness, the weather, someone's broken promise, an accident, and even death, lie within the framework of that mystery and will alter or even prevent us from carrying out our plans.

The best preparation for the future does not consist in think-

[12] Charles R. Joy, *Albert Schweitzer: An Anthology* (Boston: Beacon Press, 1947), p. 22.

ing about it or in planning for it, but in doing the work of today. The future is but the unfolding of the present. The wise farmer spends very little time thinking about the harvest at the time of seeding. His whole concern is to get the seed into the ground under the best possible conditions and to give it the best care. So far as he can control it, the future is involved in every day's work.

Spengler, the German philosopher, said: "Nations begin to deteriorate when people leave the soil." There is always that danger. Once we begin to get away from the soil there is a tendency toward intellectualism, an idolatry of reason, and a departure from the phenomenon of wonder.

Perhaps Abraham Lincoln alludes to this very thing in a poetic thought he once expressed. At a time in his early life, prior to his election as President, Lincoln practiced law in Springfield, Illinois. Feeling the need to revisit a farm near Gentry, a place he knew as home during his adolescent years, he walked the once familiar fields. After that experience he wrote: "This very ground where grew my bread that formed my bones. How strange, old fields, on thee I stand and feel I'm a part of thee."

Lincoln seems to be saying that he needed to return to the soil, to experience the "feel" of dirt under his feet, and rediscover a sense of relatedness to the overall whole.

Contact with dirt provides children with a fundamental learning experience, particularly in the planting of a garden. Digging up the soil, planting seeds, weeding, watching the first onions poke their shoots up, eventually deciding when it is time to harvest—all these things provide a learning experience for children, not to be found in any other type of experience. Not only is it fun to watch a garden grow, but the sense of personal involvement and interrelatedness with other unseen forces of nature gives to children a basic feeling of identity, of personal worth in relation to the entire cosmic life-giving process: an I'M OK—YOU'RE OK experience with the universe.

I remember my own garden as a child. One day I could no longer resist the temptation to pull up several radishes to see if they had grown big enough to eat. They hadn't, so I proceeded to tuck them carefully back into the ground and pack dirt around them. That was the end of those radishes. When one once disturbs the unseen forces within nature that are also at work in the growth of radishes, they stop growing.

Millions of children today, growing up in concrete and brick environments, will never get the opportunity to dig into dirt with their hands. Though it can look terribly messy, children are taking care of a basic need that they feel when they walk —or jump—into a mud puddle. There is no feeling like that of feeling mud squish up between one's toes.

Our search for answers to the "why" of our involvement with each other and the universe must not only include the reality of our loneliness—a basic condition of our existence— but it must *begin* at that point.

The organized religions of the world, with their codes of behavior, make loneliness their cornerstone—each in its own way spelling out those creeds that encourage men to risk loving in ways that will help them rise above their loneliness. While they all acknowledge the existence and centrality of loneliness, they differ only in their explanation as to the *reason* for it; some referring to it as but a condition of existence, others linking it to the sinful nature of men.

Buddhism: "Hurt not others with that which pains yourself."

Christianity: "All things whatsoever ye would that men should do to you do ye even so to them."

Judaism: "What is hurtful to yourself do not do to your fellow men. That is the whole of the Torah and the remainder is but commentary. Go learn it."

Hinduism: "This is the sum of duty; do naught to others which if done to thee would cause thee pain."

Islam: "No one of you is a believer until he loves for his brother what he loves for himself."

Confucianism: "Is there any maxim which ought to be acted upon through one's whole life? Surely the maxim of loving kindness is do not do unto others what you would not they do unto you."

Christianity is the only one of these major religions that says man's basic nature is such that it affects, colors, and shapes the quality of his love; hence the reason for his loneliness. The reason? Sin.

Not long ago during a church retreat at which I was lecturing I found myself holding a hymnbook with a woman and singing the words of a hymn entitled "Amazing Grace":

> Amazing Grace, how sweet the sound
> That saved a wretch like me.
> I once was blind but now am found,
> Was blind but now I see.

When the last note of the piano had faded away she turned to me and whispered, "I know I'm a long ways from being perfect . . . but a wretch?"

Evidently Calvin felt that "wretch" was the most appropriate term also: "For I do not call it humility to suppose that we have anything left. We cannot think of ourselves as we ought to think without utterly despising everything that may be supposed to be excellent in us."[13]

The point is that our view of man's basic nature spells the difference between the organized religions; the humanistic religions stress man's strengths, wisdom, reason, dependence upon self, and his basic goodness; the authoritarian religions lay emphasis on our helplessness, dependence, weakness, sin, and wretchedness.

If, then, we hold to the view that man is indeed a sinner, the reasons for our fear of love begin at the point of believing that man's basic nature is defective.

[13] John Calvin, *Institutes of the Christian Religion* (New York: Westminster Press, 1960).

Bertrand Russell, never known for his timidity, took issue with the doctrine of sin on the premise that it makes man feel inferior. "The unwise education of children by parents in the form of taboos results in the child growing 'inward' and being deprived of some normal satisfactions, particularly sexual satisfaction."[14]

Noting the difference between "committing sin" and "consciousness of sin," Russell says that man is perpetually incurring his own disapproval which, if he is religious, he interprets as being the disapproval of God.

Tartly, he equates sinning with narcissism; both of which are concerned with self-absorption—looking inward.

Sinner. Sinning has its roots in the unconscious. The individual goes through life with a sense of guilt and feeling that the best is not for him; that his highest moments are those of penitence. The source of all this is the moral teaching which the man received before he was six years old at the hand of his mother or his nurse. He learned before that age that it was wicked to swear and not quite nice to use any but ladylike language, that only bad men drink. He knew those to be the views of his mother and believed them to be those of his creator. To be affectionately treated by mother, or if she was neglectful, by his nurse, was the greatest pleasure in life, and only attainable when he had not been known to sin against the moral code. He therefore came to associate something vaguely awful with any conduct of which his mother and nurse would disapprove.

Narcissism. The habit of admiring oneself and wishing to be admired. Up to a point this is normal and not to be deplored. When vanity is carried too far there is no genuine interest in any other person and therefore no real satisfaction to be obtained from love. The man who is interested only in himself is not admirable and is not felt to be so. Vanity, when it passes beyond a point, kills the pleasure in every activity for its own sake and thus leads inevitably to boredom. A narcissist, inspired by the homage paid to great painters, becomes an art student, but as painting is for him a mere

[14] Bertrand Russell, *The Conquest of Happiness* (New York: Liveright Publishing Company, 1930).

means to an end, the technique never becomes interesting and no object can be seen except in result to self.[15]

Original sin and loneliness

Original sin stipulates that man's loneliness is not the result of something that he has personally done but that it is a condition of *being* upon birth.

In the Christian orientation "sin" means separation. The Bible addresses itself to two states of being: man's sin and God's grace. Everything in the Old and New Testaments is designed to clarify or elaborate on those two states of being. Sin is the term employed to describe man's fallen state; whereas grace is the word that most adequately conveys the nature of God's love. This grace, as exhibited in the death of Jesus, the Son of God, is portrayed as satisfying our most basic need, reconciliation. Because it is shown to be a divine reconciliation, it extends beyond this life into eternity.

In the traditional story of the fall of Adam and Eve, four results are cited:

1. Separation of man from God, the separation being characterized by the sudden onset of fear in man, fear of God's punishment. Adam and Eve ran.

2. Separation of man from man. They became afraid of one another.

3. Separation of man from himself. Separation in the sense of the discrepancy that existed between the outward image that Adam and Eve projected ("If it weren't for them") as against the fears that they were actually experiencing and feeling.

4. Separation of man from nature. After their banishment from the Garden of Eden, God is quoted as saying that the nature of work would become tedious. Man would have to work hard to earn his bread.

The original harmony that existed between God and man

[15] *Ibid.*

lay in the nature of the perfect love and trust between them. There was no fear of love. But that changed abruptly after the fall. Trust was shattered and fear abruptly made its inroads into every relationship, including man's relationship with God.

According to Christian belief, the Resurrection of Jesus Christ from the dead is the ultimate—if not the only final and absolute—answer to the reality of our aloneness and loneliness. "Love has no fear in it; instead perfect love expels fear for fear involves punishment. Therefore he who fears has not reached love's perfection. We love Him because He first loved us" (1 John 4:18–19).

Whatever our belief concerning the nature of man or the reasons for our loneliness, one thing is certain. As we become more responsible for our fear of love, our times of aloneness become less and less cluttered with debris; they become moments that we anticipate rather than dread, times out of which new appreciation, awareness, and decisions flow.

index

Inferiority, feelings of, 4
Influence, 22
Initiative, small risk, 39
Institutes of the Christian Religion
    (Calvin), 135
Intimacy, limits of, 106-107
Islam, 134

Joy, Charles R., 131-132
Judaism, 134

Letters and Papers from Prison
    (Bonhoeffer), 61
Lincoln, Abraham, 133
Listening, 99
Loneliness (Moustakas), 62
Loners, 66-69
Love, fear of, x-xii, 2, 12-13, 91-92
    and escaping responsibility,
        34-51
    and feelings of inferiority, 4
    the freeze-up, 14
    roles, 15-17
    and trust, 21-22
Loving, assuming responsibility
        for, 72-80
    learning, 78-80
    maturity, 72-74
    pain of growth and, 74-75
    super good guys and, 75-78
Lucky breaks, waiting for, 41

Man's Search for Meaning
    (Frankl), 127
Marriage and family, 90-107
    allowance for humanness, 91
    alternatives (within the family),
        99-100
    appropriate time for sharing, 106
    constructive resentments and
        appreciations, 104-106
    expectations of understanding,
        90-91
    fantasies, 92-94
    fear of love, 91-92

limits of intimacy, 106-107
parents and children, 96-97
power and authority, 100-104
teen-agers feeling misunder-
    stood, 97-98
unfinished business and, 94-96
Marshmallow strokes, 24-25
Melancholy, x
Mencken, H. L., 4
Moses, Grandma, 111
Moustakas, Clark E., 62

Nature, Man and Woman
    (Watts), 129, 130
Negative strokes, 28
Nervous breakdowns, 2
New Testament, 137
Nietzsche, Friedrich, 127
No-risk philosophy, 14-15
Nostalgia, x

Obesity, 11
OK position, the, 29-32
Old Testament, 137, 138
Original sin, 137-138

Pastimes, 83-84, 112
Personality, parent-adult-child
    concept of, xiii
Placing all eggs in one basket, 49
Powell, John, 59
Present loneliness, "I'm unlovable"
    and, 8-11
Psychoanalysis and Religion
    (Fromm), 125-126

Questions, child's, 4

React, ability to, 34, 41
Religion, xi, 124-138
    definitions of, 124-125
    development of, 129
    nature of our discontent, 127-
        129
    original sin and, 137-138